THE
WALKER'S LOG

A Daily Record
Of Your
Walking Workouts

D1793356

Leslie Carola

Longmeadow Press

Although preventative and rehabilitative exercises generally have a positive effect on your health, they are not without risk and it is, therefore, suggested that you consult with your doctor prior to the commencement of any exercise program. The author and publisher of this book assume no responsibility or liability for injury resulting from your exercise program or any activity suggested in this book.

Design: Robert Carola
Front cover photograph: Cor Videler

ISBN: 0-681-40971-1

Printed in the United States of America.

0 9 8 7 6 5 4 3 2 1

Foreword

I've been a physician for over forty years, and I have seen time and time again the relationship between a person's mental outlook and his or her physical condition. If more physicians would write prescriptions for ''one walk every day'' we would not need as many tranquilizers, sleeping pills, mood elevators, diet pills, headache cures, etc. Remember, it was Hippocrates who told us ''walking is man's best medicine.'' We simply feel better when we are physically active. We feel better both mentally and physically. And when we feel good mentally, many physical ailments disappear.

I am not underestimating real medical problems, nor am I encouraging anyone to ignore symptoms of physical distress. What I am emphasizing is that most of us would be a lot healthier, happier and generally physically fitter if we took a walk every day. It's what I tell my patients to do, and what my family and I have done for years.

So, check with your own physician, and join, with Ralph Waldo Emerson, ''...the best of humanity that goes out to walk.''

Joseph S. Rechtschaffen, M.D.
Author of *The Rechtschaffen Diet*

New York, New York
September 1989

Why Walk?

Walk your way to good health. Walking is not only an enjoyable activity, but it can be a sound personal fitness program. Walking is an exercise that can easily fit into your schedule. It requires very little skill, special equipment, or clothing. Walking will lower your blood pressure; relieve stress; strengthen leg and abdominal muscles; improve the quality of your sleep; help you to think more clearly, lose weight, reduce body fat; strengthen your cardiovascular system, and in general, will make you feel better.

Walking is the healthiest, safest aerobic exercise. It is the most natural way to build your fitness. Even if you have had an inactive lifestyle for many years, and developed some bad habits that could lead to poor health, you will improve your health quickly by following a simple walking program. And in six to eight weeks you will be noticeably trimmer, and maybe even wearing clothes one size smaller.

There is no trick to walking. You simply put one foot in front of the other, and always keep one on the ground. Walking is simple. In fact, that may be one of the reasons it has been overlooked as an exercise. It is easy, inexpensive, and fun. Exercise and fitness do not have to be complicated, expensive, or boring.

When you run, you land with a force of 3 to 4 times your body weight each time a foot hits the ground. When you play basketball or tennis or aerobic dance and leap into the air, you can land with the force of 7 times your body weight. This causes many injuries. When you walk, you land with a force of 1 and a half times your body weight. There are far fewer injuries with walking than with any other aerobic exercise.

Walking is safer than running. It places less stress on the joints and heart. Because walking is a moderate exercise, it is suitable for everyone -- young, old, overweight, underweight, weak, strong. Before beginning a walking program, be sure to discuss it with your physician.

After two weeks of consistent walking for exercise you will be a serious exerciser. Your body responds! You are stronger, have more endurance and self-confidence to continue or even proceed to a more rigorous course. Muscles are now nicely toned, and you are no longer out of breath after walking around the block.

Although we all live with stress, too much stress in our lives can be extremely damaging. Since some stress is inevitable, our goal should be to learn to cope with it and manage it. One of the easiest and most successful methods of dealing with stress is a regimen of moderate exercise three to four times a week. Regular physical activity actually changes your body chemistry.

Walking has been found to be the safest and most efficient form of exercise. Our bodies were meant to be used; the more we use them, the more efficient they are.

To sum up, walking benefits you in many ways:
- Provides aerobic conditioning
- Relieves stress
- Improves mood and clears thinking
- Aids weight loss and weight maintenance
- Slows age-related osteoporosis
- Lowers blood pressure
- Helps relieve arthritis and diabetes.

Getting Started

Before starting any fitness program, be sure to consult with your physician. You should have an honest idea what kind of shape you are in before you start. A fitness walking program produces a well-conditioned cardiovascular system. This means that the body is able to deliver plenty of oxygen to the working muscles while, simultaneously, improving the muscles' capacity to use this extra oxygen. For sustained exercise there must be a continuous oxygen supply to the muscles. That's why aerobics are important. If the muscles and cardiovascular system are poorly conditioned, you tire quickly.

There is only one way to improve the cardiovascular system and that is to exercise at the proper intensity -- the "minimum-threshold intensity." If exercise is performed below this level, there will be little or no improvement in fitness. However, when you exercise at the right intensity for your age, you will develop an improved capacity for exercise.

Learn to take your pulse so that you can monitor your resting and working heart rate. To take your pulse, jog in place for 30 seconds, then place three fingers on the inside of your wrist, on the side of your throat, or your temple. The easiest place to feel your pulse is probably on your throat, just below your jaw and next to your Adam's apple. Press gently so that you don't interrupt the flow of blood and lower the heart rate which would produce an inaccurate reading. Take a few

4

practice readings when you are rested and relaxed. You will need a watch or clock with a second hand. Count your pulse beats for 10 seconds and multiply by 6 to get a per minute pulse.

To find your theoretical maximum resting heart rate, subtract your age from 220. To increase your stamina, you should walk at an intensity between 70 and 80 percent of this maximum. Find those numbers and then divide the 70 and 80 percent numbers by 6, because we are going to determine a 10-second pulse reading.

Let's assume you are 40 years old. 220 minus forty equals 180. 70 percent of 180 is 126; and 80 percent of 180 is 144. 126 divided by 6 is 21; 144 divided by 6 is 24. If you are forty years old, your exercise pulse for 10 seconds should be between 21 and 24 beats.

It is only sensible to start any new exercise program slowly and work up to the recommended pace. One thing to remember is that you should slow down if you cannot carry on a conversation while you are walking. You should never be breathless. Breathe deeply and regularly; don't hold your breath as you walk.

For good aerobic conditioning and psychological benefits, you should walk briskly 45 minutes to an hour a day, four days a week. But begin a walking program by walking 15 minutes each day at a leisurely pace, perhaps only 2 miles per hour (mph) at the outset, especially if you are recovering from an illness or injury. For a very overweight person, 3 mph is a fast walking pace. For a person in generally good health, anything under 3 mph is slow. Normally, 4-5 mph is the optimum, brisk pace.

Walking Tips

- Walk naturally. There is no right or wrong way. With the proper shoes, anyone can walk for fitness.

- The golden rule is to do what is comfortable. Challenge yourself, but don't do too much. You should never go beyond the point where you cannot go out walking again in 24 hours.

- Exercise should be an everyday thing. Don't go out and walk 10 miles one day, just to do it, and then never do it again.

- Good posture is essential to good walking. Keep your head and chin up, stomach and buttocks tucked in. Look straight ahead, not down at the ground. Swing your arms for balance, and to give power and distance to your stride.

- If there are no sidewalks where you are walking, walk on the side of the street facing the traffic. You want to be able to see the oncoming cars. If there is no sidewalk or shoulder to walk on, stay as close to the edge of the road as possible.

- Where you walk, and what you walk on, are important. You will have greater endurance, less leg fatigue and fewer problems with shin pains if you walk on relatively soft ground (such as grass, dirt, or packed pine needles). Try to select a smooth, level surface.

- If you walk at night, a flashlight would be helpful, for you to see a dark path, or for oncoming cars to be aware of you on the road. A reflective vest is a necessity for night-walking.

- A walking stick of any kind is useful for keeping your balance, or for warding off unfriendly dogs. The stick can be anything from the perfect carved ivory walking stick to a piece of a branch found along the road.

- Remember to stop walking before you are exhausted.

- The easiest way to find a course is to drive a mile in your car, then walk that mile and time yourself.

- The only exercise that works is one that keeps your interest. You might try to make a chart of varying routes, and then walk a different route whenever you want a change of scene.

- Find a comfortable but brisk rhythm. Take smooth, long strides to help you walk straight and to stretch your muscles.

- You can always walk indoors if the weather is bad or if you feel uncomfortable or unsafe on the streets. Many people walk in shopping malls. In fact, there are an estimated 500,000 ''mall walkers'' across the country. With this in mind, a major athletic shoe company is developing a walking shoe for use on the hard, slick surfaces of indoor shopping malls.

- Set up a walking club at your office to walk during breaks and at your lunch hour. It has been shown that the exercise boosts morale and increases energy, efficiency, and creativity.

- Keep track of your distance and time, heartbeat and weight. A written record of your progress is invaluable.

Warm-Up

Muscles can damage easily. You must warm them up before beginning, and cool them down after any exercise. Exercise that is too sudden, severe, long, or even too frequent, will cause stiff, sore muscles if the body is not prepared. Actually, any vigorous exercise will cause pain if the body is not properly acclimated.

Warming up raises the temperature of the body's tissues, which makes it less likely that you will pull or tear muscles or tendons. Spend five to ten minutes warming up. The earlier in the day you walk, the longer you should warm-up. Ten minutes is best in the morning while your muscles are still a bit stiff. Five minutes would probably be enough before a walk at the end of the day when your muscles are already warm and flexible from the day's activities.

 The warm-up gets the blood flowing to the muscles, preparing them to work. You should not really stretch your muscles before a walk, but rather gently move and flex them. The cool-down after your walk is the time to stretch the muscles. The warm-up period allows the heart to slowly speed up before the aerobic part of the workout. It allows you time to relax and focus on exercise and breathing.

By beginning slowly and gradually increasing the intensity of the exercise, the heart, lungs, muscles, and joints adapt to the increasing activity. A proper warm-up increases the elasticity of the muscles, tendons and ligaments.

You can warm up the whole body with heat, by taking a bath, for example. Or you can perform a series of calisthenics to provide general muscle warm-up. Or you can walk at half- to three-quarters pace. All three types of warm-ups are acceptable as a prelude to walking, but the specific muscular walking is best. It warms up the very muscles and ligaments that will be contracting and relaxing at the rate of twice per second for a full 30 or 40 minutes during the walk. It also indicates the coordination and balance needed in the walk. Start your warm-up with a few minutes of gentle strolling followed by five minutes of more vigorous walking. You will then be prepared for a brisk pace in the actual walking workout. Walking turns out to be the best warm-up for walking.

Remember that the warm-up does not count as part of the walk. The warm-up and cool-down are in addition to the actual brisk walk.

Walking uses only a few major muscle groups. If you do choose to stretch before walking, you only need to work on the muscles of the buttocks and the hamstring and calf muscles of the legs, since those are the muscles used most in walking.

Cool·Down

The cool-down is just the warm-up in reverse. Instead of preparing your body for activity, you are preparing it to return to its normal working level. While you are exercising, your heart pumps blood at a fast rate to supply the active muscles with more oxygen. When you suddenly stop exercising, your heart continues to beat at an accelerated pace for a while. But the muscles are no longer active, and therefore an excess amount of blood may temporarily collect in the muscles and veins, resulting in light-headedness or chills. A cooling-down period of gentle exercise allows your heart to slow down gradually.

Cool down gradually. Let all the body systems settle down evenly. During a workout, your body undergoes many changes: the blood flow to the muscles increases greatly; the muscles of the legs, by contracting rhythmically, help pump the blood back to the heart. In response to the increased amount of blood return, the heart pumps faster and more vigorously.

If you do want to stretch gently after your walking workout walk slowly for about five minutes and then start slowly stretching your muscles. The purpose of stretching is to lengthen the muscle fibers, and hold them at that length until they are conditioned not to go into a spasm if they tire. Start a stretch slowly; hold it for 30 seconds, and then release it slowly.

Cool down by walking slowly for a few minutes, or sit down on the ground with your legs stretched out in front of you so that the blood does not have to flow uphill to return to the heart from the legs. Don't take a hot shower or bath immediately after exercising. Heat brings more blood to the surface, leaving less for the heart to pump to the vital organs. Without sufficient blood reaching the brain, you could faint.

A few gentle stretches:

Shoulder shrugs to loosen shoulder, upper back and neck muscles:
- Stand straight with arms at sides. Bring shoulders straight up as if trying to touch your ears with them.
- Lower shoulders when you feel a tightening in the shoulder muscles, and in the lower shoulders.
- 10 repetitions at a slow, steady pace.

Half-squats to get blood flowing to leg muscles:
- Stand straight, with hands on hips. Bend knees halfway,   and sink into a half-squat. Keep your back straight, feet on the ground.
- Straighten legs and stand erect. Squat once every two to three seconds 10-15 times. Movements should be slow and smooth.
- Steady yourself by holding onto the back of a chair, if necessary.

Abdominal curls for stomach muscles:
- Lie on back, with knees bent, and feet flat on floor.
- Fold hands across chest. Curl body up slowly to a 30^0 angle, starting by moving head forward and then bringing the rest of your body up, vertebra by vertebra.
- Return smoothly and slowly, vertebra by vertebra. Do not bring your body all the way up to a sitting position.
- Do 10-15 repetitions at a slow, steady pace.

Overhead reaches.
- Stand straight with arms at sides. Reach one arm slowly up into the air above your head.
- Bring the raised arm down slowly while reaching up slowly with the other arm.
- Make the motion smooth and gentle.
- Continue for one minute.

Nutrition and Weight Loss

When you are involved in an exercise program, you should pay special attention to your diet. You may wish to lose some weight or simply improve your health. Whatever the reason, you should be eating properly, that is, a well-balanced diet including foods from the three major food groups -- proteins, carbohydrates, and fats. Proteins are the muscle builders, carbohydrates give you the energy you need, and small amounts of fats are essential for digestion and healthy skin and hair. We need foods from each of these groups every day. Your body will perform better, you will feel better, and your mood will be stable.

In order to lose weight, you must take in fewer calories by eating than you expend in energy. In other words, you need to have a calorie deficit at the end of the day. As we know, exercise burns calories, but you must still be aware of how much you eat and what you eat. In order to have the energy to exercise well, and to reap the benefits of your exercise program, your body needs proper nutrition.

One of the most significant ways to control your food intake is to monitor food portions. Eating too much of anything will add unwanted fat to your body. And what a waste it would be if you spend your energy on a healthy exercise program and then defeat yourself by eating too much food.

Exercise does not increase your appetite. In fact, many walkers have found that a good long walk decreases their appetites, especially for foods with high sugar and fat content. A juicy, crisp apple is always delicious, but somehow after a brisk walk, it tastes even better. Chances are if you are walking at least three to four times a week, you will not want to overeat. If you start your day with a healthy breakfast of fruit and whole grain bread, cereal, or pasta you will have energy for the day.

To lose weight:
- Eat small to moderate meals three to four times a day.
- Eat fresh fruit in the morning; vegetables, salad, bread and a small amount of protein for lunch; and a small amount of protein, vegetables, salad for dinner. No more than 15 percent of your total daily calories should be protein. Eat fresh fruit for snacks whenever possible, and when given a choice always choose a whole fruit over juice. Whole fruit has more fiber, which aids digestion.
- Try not to eat after 8 PM.
- Limit caffeine drinks (coffee, tea, soda) to 2 per day.
- Remove skin from poultry before cooking to avoid excess fat in your diet.
- Use no more than two tablespoons of dressing on your salad. Avoid creamy dressings with buttermilk and sour cream. Olive oil vinaigrette is delicious and healthy.
- Limit your intake of sweets to no more than two or three small servings per week.
- Limit the amount of alcohol you drink to a maximum of 1½ ounces. of liquor, 12 ounces of beer or 6 ounces of wine per day. It is best if you limit the times you drink alcohol to two or three days per week.
- You don't have to eat food just because it is being served. You can say "no" to a heavy dinner with chocolate mousse for dessert. You are the one to choose what you will eat.

Varying your caloric intake is essential to setting and maintaining an active metabolism. Slight periodic increases in calories during a diet actually *boost* your metabolism and lead to a more consistent weight loss in the long run. If you maintain a low-calorie diet week after week, your body stores extra calories to combat the famine-like environment thus lowering your metabolism and slowing down your weight loss. You don't want this to happen. One of the purposes of exercising is to speed up your metabolism.

Complex carbohydrates (whole grain breads and pasta, fresh fruits and vegetables) are the primary energy source for your body, and the greatest number of calories you eat each day should come from this group. The average-sized woman needs about 46 grams of protein each day, while a man needs about 56 grams.

A healthy plan would be to have two poultry, two vegetable, two fish and one red meat dinners per week. Meatless dinners are not deprivation meals: pasta with fresh vegetables is a wonderfully tasty, satisfying meal any time.

A high intake of complex carbohydrates and a vigorous exercise program will automatically help you control any craving for sweets. High-fiber foods (complex carbohydrates) will give you long-term energy and also move food quickly through your intestinal tract. Speeding up the time food remains in your body is beneficial to your health. Water is an essential nutrient for the body. Our bodies are two-thirds water. To maintain a proper liquid balance, be sure to drink water before and after your walk. And if you are walking in very hot or humid weather, bring some water along with you to drink enroute. You should drink eight 8-ounce glasses of water every day.

Motivate
Yourself

- Even if you feel tentative about taking a walk, put on your exercise clothes and shoes, and go outside for five minutes. Chances are, once you've started your walk, you will continue with pleasure.
- Imagine what you will look like in a year if you keep up with your walking program.
- Promise yourself an extravagant treat if you meet your exercise goals.
- Think of yourself as an active person in control of your body. Visualize yourself walking.
- Know yourself. Choose your exercise time carefully. The time you take to exercise will make you more productive, and feel better and more alive.
- If you feel your motivation is weak, join a walking club or enlist a few friends to walk with you.
- Consider exercise a choice rather than a duty. It is your gift to yourself.
- Add music to your walking. Take a walk with your Walkman.
- *Some* exercise is better than *no* exercise. Don't give up the whole program if you miss one or two days of walking.
- Set goals for yourself, both short- and long-term. Record your progress.

15

For Women Only

Because men tend to have more body mass and muscle tissue than women do, they generally burn calories at a faster rate. (Women tend to burn about 500 fewer calories per day than men do.) Ideally, a man's body contains 15-20 percent fat, whereas a woman's body usually contains about 20-25 percent body fat (and therefore less muscle). Muscle is metabolically much more active than fat tissue. Even inactive muscle burns more calories than fat does. Therefore, there is a correlation between the amount of muscle tissue in your body and your basal metabolic rate. The more muscle and the less fat you have, the more you can eat without gaining weight. Walking for fitness will help you burn off fat and increase muscle tissue.

Age is also a factor affecting metabolism in both men and women. As we age, we may be less physically active, and throughout the aging process, we lose lean body mass. You may lose less body mass if you exercise.

Women's bodies store extra fat to provide a healthy, nutritious environment for a fetus. Unless your physician has specific restrictions for you, there is no reason not to continue or even start a fitness walking program during pregnancy. But do be sure to discuss any fitness program with your physician before starting.

Exercise during pregnancy will keep your stamina high, your spirits up, and the muscles in your back strong and flexible, providing extra support for the baby. The American College of Obstetrics and Gynecology recommends walking for pregnant women as long as the pulse rate does not exceed 140 beats per minute for more than 15 minutes. You may therefore need to modify your more vigorous workout to a more leisurely one.

During pregnancy a woman needs about 15 percent more calories than usual during the first trimester and probably twice that in the latter two trimesters. A weight gain during pregnancy is normal. It is not the time to diet to lose weight (unless your physician has put you on a special reducing diet); your body needs the extra nutrients. Do not eat junk food, though. Dieting to lose weight can lead to unnecessarily low birth weight for the baby.

The time and pressure constraints of running a home and managing a successful career and family can be devastating. Studies have shown that the combination of work and family responsibilities puts more stress on women than on men. As you know, walking combats stress. Walking is a natural tranquilizer.

Walking for exercise is beneficial and healthful to the older woman.By age 60, about 20 percent of women and 5 percent of men have osteoporosis. Although both men and women experience bone weakening, women are more likely to have greater problems. Participation in a walking program is the only known natural, safe way to effectively increase bone mass. Of course, the most important nutritional requirement is a calcium-rich diet or calcium supplements taken at the direction of your physician.

The metabolic changes that occur as a result of a walking program will help to make women lean and trim without extreme dieting. Walking will also decrease high blood pressure, and strengthen your bone structure. The biochemical changes as a result of walking will give you a mental boost, reduce anxiety and depression, and improve carbohydrate and fat metabolism.

Wear
and Care

Walking is probably the least expensive fitness exercise. Basically, all you need is a good pair of shoes made of a natural substance, designed specifically for walking. Ordinary sneakers or running shoes will not give you enough foot support. You could wear hiking boots if you are taking an especially long hike or walking trip. If you walk every day, or walk more than an hour a day, you should have two pairs of walking shoes so that you will always have one dry pair available. You should never wear wet shoes to go walking.

In choosing a walking shoe, you should look for one that will give you both support and comfort. Loafers are comfortable, but give you no support; heavy work boots give you support, but very little comfort. A walking shoe should have additional support and cushion around the heel and sole. You should not wear the same pair of shoes every day. Give your shoes a chance to air out. Every week, loosen the laces, open them up as much as possible and put them in the sun. The sunlight removes a tremendous amount of bacteria which could corrode the shoes. You could even vacuum the inside of your shoes.

There should be at least ¼ to ½ inch of room between your longest toe and the front of the shoe. You should be able to wiggle your toes and spread them out comfortably. It is essential to wear socks, to prevent blisters. You should always wear absorbent socks to protect your feet and shoes. Cotton socks are the most absorbent, although woolen socks are also acceptable. Socks do not have to be thick, but they should cushion your foot from rough terrain. In cold weather, wear two pairs of socks: they protect your feet from blisters, provide a cushion and absorb perspiration. Be sure to wear clean socks; dirty ones contribute to blisters and athlete's foot.

The most sensible way to dress for walking is in natural-fiber shorts and T-shirt, or a warm-up suit. Never wear rubberized clothing to walk in. A large, roomy cotton T-shirt, cotton socks and walking shoes is an appropriate outfit for warm weather. Avoid tight elastic bands on wrists, ankles, and waist. Loose, slightly flared-leg shorts, or loose-fitting sweat pants are appropriate.

In cold weather, layered clothing is the key to staying warm. Several light layers trap warm body heat and act as a natural heating system with your own body warmth. A water- and/or windproof jacket is preferable in rainy or snowy cold weather. On the very coldest days, you may want to wear thermal underwear under your sweat pants. It soaks up the perspiration, leaving your skin dry and warm. For cold weather, light woolen gloves or mittens are necessary. On wet days, you can even add a pair of waterproof nylon gloves or mittens over the woolen ones. In very cold weather, or in cold, wet weather, wearing a hat is a good idea. You lose about 30 percent of your body heat through your head. A woolen hat keeps you warm, and if you pull it down over your forehead you can protect yourself from cold, wet blasts and resultant sinus infections.

For warm or cold weather, loose layered clothing is appropriate. You want to stay comfortable and dry. Clothes of natural fibers (wool and cotton) are best next to your body.

Never let bad weather, or the fact that you don't have the right clothes or equipment prevent you from taking a walk. Buy a pair of walking shoes, and walk away!

Goals for the week Improve pace to 4.0 mph. Increase time to 1 hour at 4 mph pace.

SUNDAY

Pulse 123   Weight 135   Time 7 (AM) PM

Weather / Temperature cool & damp   Course 3.5 miles /

Distance 3.5 miles   Time 1 hour   Pace (mph) 3.5

COMMENTS Felt energetic, able to move from 45 mins to 1 hr time easily.

MONDAY

Pulse _____   Weight _____   Time _____ AM PM

Weather / Temperature _____   Course _____

Distance _____   Time _____   Pace (mph) _____

COMMENTS No walk today. Raining.

TUESDAY

Pulse 128   Weight _____   Time 6 AM (PM)

Weather / Temperature cool   Course hilly

Distance 3.5   Time 55 mins.   Pace (mph) 3.4

COMMENTS Tired after day's work. Confident I can increase pace. Pesky dog en route.

WEDNESDAY

Pulse 130   Weight 134.5   Time 7 (AM) PM

Weather / Temperature Lovely. cool & dry   Course short, easy.

Distance 2 mi   Time 30 mins   Pace (mph) 4.

COMMENTS Beautiful day. In rush to get to work.

THURSDAY

Pulse __135__   Weight __134__   Time __7__ (AM) PM

Weather / Temperature __cool. Dry__   Course __hilly__

Distance __3.5__   Time __45 mins__   Pace (mph) __4.0__

COMMENTS __Felt great. Beautiful day. Energized.__

FRIDAY

Pulse __135__   Weight __134__   Time __7__ (AM) PM

Weather / Temperature __Light showers - cool__   Course __Flat / easy__

Distance __4 mi.__   Time __1 hr.__   Pace (mph) __4.0__

COMMENTS __In hurry to get to work - hectic schedule.__
__Walk felt great, though.__

SATURDAY

Pulse __135__   Weight __133.5__   Time __9__ (AM) PM

Weather / Temperature __Showers - cool__   Course __Indoors - flat.__

Distance __4 mi.__   Time __1 hr.__   Pace (mph) __4.0__

COMMENTS __Tried walking in the shopping__
__mall. What a great idea!__

WEEK SUMMARY

Beginning weight __135__   Time ____ AM PM

Weight loss (week) __1.5__   (month) __5__   (year) __18__

Distance __20.5__   (month) __68__   (year) __408__

Average daily distance this week __2.9__   (this month) __2.3__

COMMENTS __Feel great. Walking helps keep me on__
__diet & helps concentration.__

DISTANCE (MILES) chart — S M T W T F S

PACE (MPH) chart — S M T W T F S

Goals for the week _____
_____
_____

SUNDAY

Pulse _____ Weight _____ Time _____ AM PM

Weather / Temperature _____ Course _____

Distance _____ Time _____ Pace (mph)_____

COMMENTS _____
_____

MONDAY

Pulse _____ Weight _____ Time _____ AM PM

Weather / Temperature _____ Course _____

Distance _____ Time _____ Pace (mph)_____

COMMENTS _____
_____

TUESDAY

Pulse _____ Weight _____ Time _____ AM PM

Weather / Temperature _____ Course _____

Distance _____ Time _____ Pace (mph)_____

COMMENTS _____
_____

WEDNESDAY

Pulse _____ Weight _____ Time _____ AM PM

Weather / Temperature _____ Course _____

Distance _____ Time _____ Pace (mph)_____

COMMENTS _____
_____

THURSDAY

Pulse _____ Weight _____ Time _____ AM PM

Weather / Temperature _____ Course _____

Distance _____ Time _____ Pace (mph)_____

COMMENTS _____

_____

FRIDAY

Pulse _____ Weight _____ Time _____ AM PM

Weather / Temperature _____ Course _____

Distance _____ Time _____ Pace (mph)_____

COMMENTS _____

_____

SATURDAY

Pulse _____ Weight _____ Time _____ AM PM

Weather / Temperature _____ Course _____

Distance _____ Time _____ Pace (mph)_____

COMMENTS _____

_____

WEEK SUMMARY

Beginning weight _____ Time _____ AM PM

Weight loss (week) _____ (month) _____ (year) _____

Distance _____ (month) _____ (year) _____

Average daily distance this week _____ (this month) _____

COMMENTS _____

_____

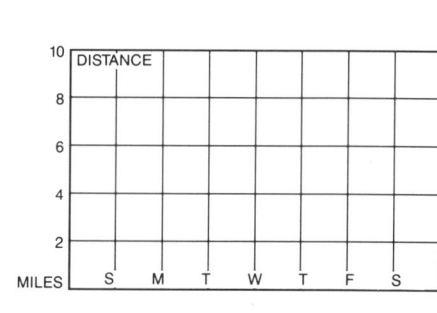

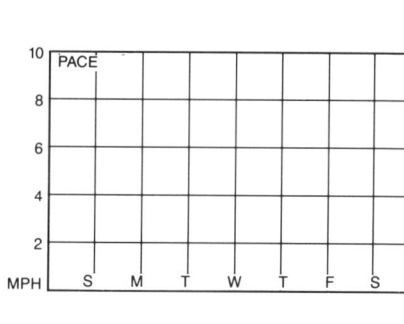

 **WEEK** _____ **2**

Goals for the week _____

_____

_____

SUNDAY

Pulse _____ Weight _____ Time _____ AM PM

Weather / Temperature _____ Course _____

Distance _____ Time _____ Pace (mph)_____

COMMENTS _____

_____

MONDAY

Pulse _____ Weight _____ Time _____ AM PM

Weather / Temperature _____ Course _____

Distance _____ Time _____ Pace (mph)_____

COMMENTS _____

_____

TUESDAY

Pulse _____ Weight _____ Time _____ AM PM

Weather / Temperature _____ Course _____

Distance _____ Time _____ Pace (mph)_____

COMMENTS _____

_____

WEDNESDAY

Pulse _____ Weight _____ Time _____ AM PM

Weather / Temperature _____ Course _____

Distance _____ Time _____ Pace (mph)_____

COMMENTS _____

_____

Pulse _____ Weight _____ Time _____ AM PM

Weather / Temperature _____ Course _____

Distance _____ Time _____ Pace (mph)_____

COMMENTS _____

_____

Pulse _____ Weight _____ Time _____ AM PM

Weather / Temperature _____ Course _____

Distance _____ Time _____ Pace (mph)_____

COMMENTS _____

_____

Pulse _____ Weight _____ Time _____ AM PM

Weather / Temperature _____ Course _____

Distance _____ Time _____ Pace (mph)_____

COMMENTS _____

_____

Beginning weight _____ Time _____ AM PM

Weight loss (week) _____ (month) _____ (year) _____

Distance _____ (month) _____ (year) _____

Average daily distance this week _____ (this month) _____

COMMENTS _____

_____

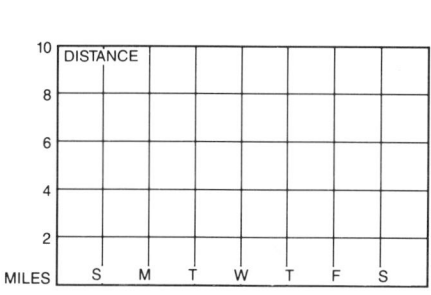

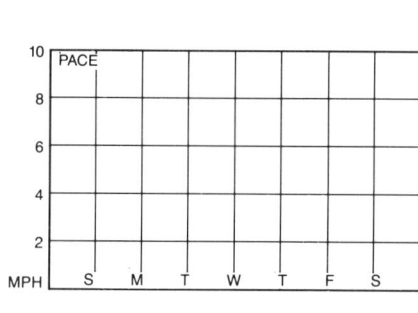

 WEEK _____ **3**

Goals for the week _____
_____
_____

SUNDAY

Pulse _____ Weight _____ Time _____ AM PM

Weather / Temperature _____ Course _____

Distance _____ Time _____ Pace (mph)_____

COMMENTS _____
_____

MONDAY

Pulse _____ Weight _____ Time _____ AM PM

Weather / Temperature _____ Course _____

Distance _____ Time _____ Pace (mph)_____

COMMENTS _____
_____

TUESDAY

Pulse _____ Weight _____ Time _____ AM PM

Weather / Temperature _____ Course _____

Distance _____ Time _____ Pace (mph)_____

COMMENTS _____
_____

WEDNESDAY

Pulse _____ Weight _____ Time _____ AM PM

Weather / Temperature _____ Course _____

Distance _____ Time _____ Pace (mph)_____

COMMENTS _____
_____

THURSDAY

Pulse _____ Weight _____ Time _____ AM PM

Weather / Temperature _____ Course _____

Distance _____ Time _____ Pace (mph)_____

COMMENTS _____

_____

FRIDAY

Pulse _____ Weight _____ Time _____ AM PM

Weather / Temperature _____ Course _____

Distance _____ Time _____ Pace (mph)_____

COMMENTS _____

_____

SATURDAY

Pulse _____ Weight _____ Time _____ AM PM

Weather / Temperature _____ Course _____

Distance _____ Time _____ Pace (mph)_____

COMMENTS _____

_____

WEEK SUMMARY

Beginning weight _____ Time _____ AM PM

Weight loss (week) _____ (month) _____ (year) _____

Distance _____ (month) _____ (year) _____

Average daily distance this week _____ (this month) _____

COMMENTS _____

_____

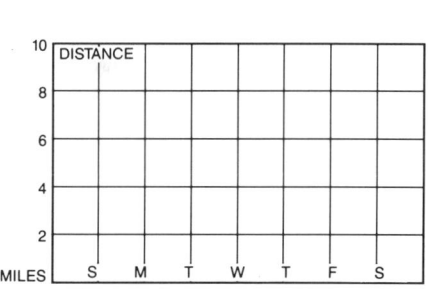

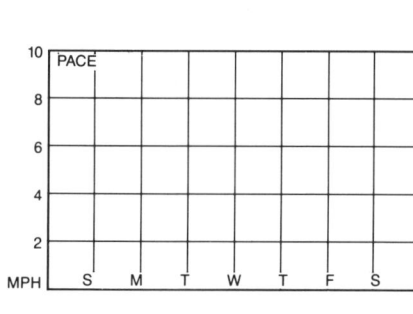

 **WEEK** _____ **4**

Goals for the week _____
_____
_____

SUNDAY

Pulse _____ Weight _____ Time _____ AM PM

Weather / Temperature _____ Course _____

Distance _____ Time _____ Pace (mph)_____

COMMENTS _____
_____

MONDAY

Pulse _____ Weight _____ Time _____ AM PM

Weather / Temperature _____ Course _____

Distance _____ Time _____ Pace (mph)_____

COMMENTS _____
_____

TUESDAY

Pulse _____ Weight _____ Time _____ AM PM

Weather / Temperature _____ Course _____

Distance _____ Time _____ Pace (mph)_____

COMMENTS _____
_____

WEDNESDAY

Pulse _____ Weight _____ Time _____ AM PM

Weather / Temperature _____ Course _____

Distance _____ Time _____ Pace (mph)_____

COMMENTS _____
_____

Pulse _____ Weight _____ Time _____ AM PM

Weather / Temperature _____ Course _____

Distance _____ Time _____ Pace (mph)_____

COMMENTS _____

_____

Pulse _____ Weight _____ Time _____ AM PM

Weather / Temperature _____ Course _____

Distance _____ Time _____ Pace (mph)_____

COMMENTS _____

_____

Pulse _____ Weight _____ Time _____ AM PM

Weather / Temperature _____ Course _____

Distance _____ Time _____ Pace (mph)_____

COMMENTS _____

_____

Beginning weight _____ Time _____ AM PM

Weight loss (week) _____ (month) _____ (year) _____

Distance _____ (month) _____ (year) _____

Average daily distance this week _____ (this month) _____

COMMENTS _____

_____

DISTANCE — MILES: S M T W T F S (scale 2, 4, 6, 8, 10)

PACE — MPH: S M T W T F S (scale 2, 4, 6, 8, 10)

 **WEEK**_____ **5**

Goals for the week _____

_____

_____

SUNDAY

Pulse _____ Weight _____ Time _____ AM PM

Weather / Temperature _____ Course _____

Distance _____ Time _____ Pace (mph)_____

COMMENTS _____

_____

MONDAY

Pulse _____ Weight _____ Time _____ AM PM

Weather / Temperature _____ Course _____

Distance _____ Time _____ Pace (mph)_____

COMMENTS _____

_____

TUESDAY

Pulse _____ Weight _____ Time _____ AM PM

Weather / Temperature _____ Course _____

Distance _____ Time _____ Pace (mph)_____

COMMENTS _____

_____

WEDNESDAY

Pulse _____ Weight _____ Time _____ AM PM

Weather / Temperature _____ Course _____

Distance _____ Time _____ Pace (mph)_____

COMMENTS _____

_____

THURSDAY

Pulse _____ Weight _____ Time _____ AM PM

Weather / Temperature _____ Course _____

Distance _____ Time _____ Pace (mph)_____

COMMENTS_____

_____

FRIDAY

Pulse _____ Weight _____ Time _____ AM PM

Weather / Temperature _____ Course _____

Distance _____ Time _____ Pace (mph)_____

COMMENTS_____

_____

SATURDAY

Pulse _____ Weight _____ Time _____ AM PM

Weather / Temperature _____ Course _____

Distance _____ Time _____ Pace (mph)_____

COMMENTS_____

_____

WEEK SUMMARY

Beginning weight _____ Time _____ AM PM

Weight loss (week) _____ (month) _____ (year) _____

Distance _____ (month) _____ (year) _____

Average daily distance this week _____ (this month) _____

COMMENTS_____

_____

DISTANCE

10							
8							
6							
4							
2							
MILES	S	M	T	W	T	F	S

PACE

10							
8							
6							
4							
2							
MPH	S	M	T	W	T	F	S

 **WEEK** _____ **6**

Goals for the week _____
_____
_____

SUNDAY

Pulse _____ Weight _____ Time _____ AM PM

Weather / Temperature _____ Course _____

Distance _____ Time _____ Pace (mph)_____

COMMENTS _____
_____

MONDAY

Pulse _____ Weight _____ Time _____ AM PM

Weather / Temperature _____ Course _____

Distance _____ Time _____ Pace (mph)_____

COMMENTS _____
_____

TUESDAY

Pulse _____ Weight _____ Time _____ AM PM

Weather / Temperature _____ Course _____

Distance _____ Time _____ Pace (mph)_____

COMMENTS _____
_____

WEDNESDAY

Pulse _____ Weight _____ Time _____ AM PM

Weather / Temperature _____ Course _____

Distance _____ Time _____ Pace (mph)_____

COMMENTS _____
_____

Pulse _____ Weight _____ Time _____ AM PM

Weather / Temperature _____ Course _____

Distance _____ Time _____ Pace (mph)_____

COMMENTS _____

_____

Pulse _____ Weight _____ Time _____ AM PM

Weather / Temperature _____ Course _____

Distance _____ Time _____ Pace (mph)_____

COMMENTS _____

_____

Pulse _____ Weight _____ Time _____ AM PM

Weather / Temperature _____ Course _____

Distance _____ Time _____ Pace (mph)_____

COMMENTS _____

_____

Beginning weight _____ Time _____ AM PM

Weight loss (week) _____ (month) _____ (year) _____

Distance _____ (month) _____ (year) _____

Average daily distance this week _____ (this month) _____

COMMENTS _____

_____

DISTANCE — MILES: S M T W T F S

PACE — MPH: S M T W T F S

 **WEEK** _____ **7**

Goals for the week _____
_____
_____

SUNDAY

Pulse _____ Weight _____ Time _____ AM PM

Weather / Temperature _____ Course _____

Distance _____ Time _____ Pace (mph)_____

COMMENTS _____
_____

MONDAY

Pulse _____ Weight _____ Time _____ AM PM

Weather / Temperature _____ Course _____

Distance _____ Time _____ Pace (mph)_____

COMMENTS _____
_____

TUESDAY

Pulse _____ Weight _____ Time _____ AM PM

Weather / Temperature _____ Course _____

Distance _____ Time _____ Pace (mph)_____

COMMENTS _____
_____

WEDNESDAY

Pulse _____ Weight _____ Time _____ AM PM

Weather / Temperature _____ Course _____

Distance _____ Time _____ Pace (mph)_____

COMMENTS _____
_____

THURSDAY

Pulse _____ Weight _____ Time _____ AM PM

Weather / Temperature _____ Course _____

Distance _____ Time _____ Pace (mph)_____

COMMENTS _____

_____

FRIDAY

Pulse _____ Weight _____ Time _____ AM PM

Weather / Temperature _____ Course _____

Distance _____ Time _____ Pace (mph)_____

COMMENTS _____

_____

SATURDAY

Pulse _____ Weight _____ Time _____ AM PM

Weather / Temperature _____ Course _____

Distance _____ Time _____ Pace (mph)_____

COMMENTS _____

_____

WEEK SUMMARY

Beginning weight _____ Time _____ AM PM

Weight loss (week) _____ (month) _____ (year) _____

Distance _____ (month) _____ (year) _____

Average daily distance this week _____ (this month) _____

COMMENTS _____

_____

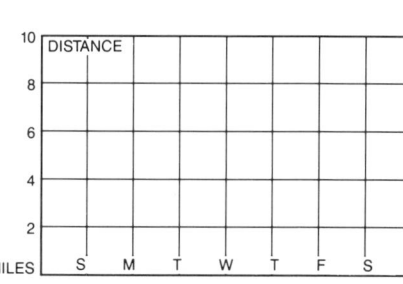

WEEK _____ **8**

Goals for the week _____
_____
_____

SUNDAY

Pulse _____ Weight _____ Time _____ AM PM

Weather / Temperature _____ Course _____

Distance _____ Time _____ Pace (mph) _____

COMMENTS _____
_____

MONDAY

Pulse _____ Weight _____ Time _____ AM PM

Weather / Temperature _____ Course _____

Distance _____ Time _____ Pace (mph) _____

COMMENTS _____
_____

TUESDAY

Pulse _____ Weight _____ Time _____ AM PM

Weather / Temperature _____ Course _____

Distance _____ Time _____ Pace (mph) _____

COMMENTS _____
_____

WEDNESDAY

Pulse _____ Weight _____ Time _____ AM PM

Weather / Temperature _____ Course _____

Distance _____ Time _____ Pace (mph) _____

COMMENTS _____
_____

THURSDAY

Pulse _____ Weight _____ Time _____ AM PM

Weather / Temperature _____ Course _____

Distance _____ Time _____ Pace (mph)_____

COMMENTS _____

_____

FRIDAY

Pulse _____ Weight _____ Time _____ AM PM

Weather / Temperature _____ Course _____

Distance _____ Time _____ Pace (mph)_____

COMMENTS _____

_____

SATURDAY

Pulse _____ Weight _____ Time _____ AM PM

Weather / Temperature _____ Course _____

Distance _____ Time _____ Pace (mph)_____

COMMENTS _____

_____

WEEK SUMMARY

Beginning weight _____ Time _____ AM PM

Weight loss (week) _____ (month) _____ (year) _____

Distance _____ (month) _____ (year) _____

Average daily distance this week _____ (this month) _____

COMMENTS _____

_____

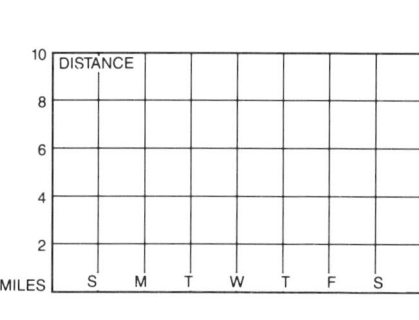

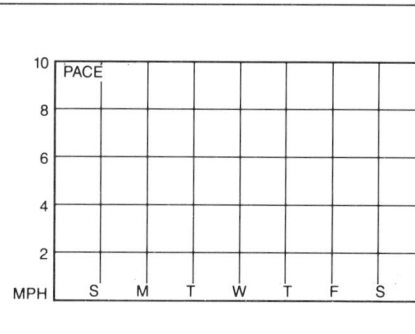

 **WEEK**_____ **9**

Goals for the week _____
_____
_____

SUNDAY

Pulse _____ Weight _____ Time _____ AM PM

Weather / Temperature _____ Course _____

Distance _____ Time _____ Pace (mph)_____

COMMENTS _____
_____

MONDAY

Pulse _____ Weight _____ Time _____ AM PM

Weather / Temperature _____ Course _____

Distance _____ Time _____ Pace (mph)_____

COMMENTS _____
_____

TUESDAY

Pulse _____ Weight _____ Time _____ AM PM

Weather / Temperature _____ Course _____

Distance _____ Time _____ Pace (mph)_____

COMMENTS _____
_____

WEDNESDAY

Pulse _____ Weight _____ Time _____ AM PM

Weather / Temperature _____ Course _____

Distance _____ Time _____ Pace (mph)_____

COMMENTS _____
_____

THURSDAY

Pulse _____ Weight _____ Time _____ AM PM

Weather / Temperature _____ Course _____

Distance _____ Time _____ Pace (mph)_____

COMMENTS _____

_____

FRIDAY

Pulse _____ Weight _____ Time _____ AM PM

Weather / Temperature _____ Course _____

Distance _____ Time _____ Pace (mph)_____

COMMENTS _____

_____

SATURDAY

Pulse _____ Weight _____ Time _____ AM PM

Weather / Temperature _____ Course _____

Distance _____ Time _____ Pace (mph)_____

COMMENTS _____

_____

WEEK SUMMARY

Beginning weight _____ Time _____ AM PM

Weight loss (week) _____ (month) _____ (year) _____

Distance _____ (month) _____ (year) _____

Average daily distance this week _____ (this month) _____

COMMENTS _____

_____

DISTANCE

10						
8						
6						
4						
2						
MILES	S	M	T	W	T	F	S

PACE

10						
8						
6						
4						
2						
MPH	S	M	T	W	T	F	S

 **WEEK**_____ **10**

Goals for the week _____
_____
_____

SUNDAY

Pulse _____ Weight _____ Time _____ AM PM

Weather / Temperature _____ Course _____

Distance _____ Time _____ Pace (mph)_____

COMMENTS _____
_____

MONDAY

Pulse _____ Weight _____ Time _____ AM PM

Weather / Temperature _____ Course _____

Distance _____ Time _____ Pace (mph)_____

COMMENTS _____
_____

TUESDAY

Pulse _____ Weight _____ Time _____ AM PM

Weather / Temperature _____ Course _____

Distance _____ Time _____ Pace (mph)_____

COMMENTS _____
_____

WEDNESDAY

Pulse _____ Weight _____ Time _____ AM PM

Weather / Temperature _____ Course _____

Distance _____ Time _____ Pace (mph)_____

COMMENTS _____
_____

THURSDAY

Pulse _____ Weight _____ Time _____ AM PM

Weather / Temperature _____ Course _____

Distance _____ Time _____ Pace (mph)_____

COMMENTS _____
_____

FRIDAY

Pulse _____ Weight _____ Time _____ AM PM

Weather / Temperature _____ Course _____

Distance _____ Time _____ Pace (mph)_____

COMMENTS _____
_____

SATURDAY

Pulse _____ Weight _____ Time _____ AM PM

Weather / Temperature _____ Course _____

Distance _____ Time _____ Pace (mph)_____

COMMENTS _____
_____

WEEK SUMMARY

Beginning weight _____ Time _____ AM PM

Weight loss (week) _____ (month) _____ (year) _____

Distance _____ (month) _____ (year) _____

Average daily distance this week _____ (this month) _____

COMMENTS _____
_____

DISTANCE
10
8
6
4
2
MILES   S   M   T   W   T   F   S

PACE
10
8
6
4
2
MPH   S   M   T   W   T   F   S

WEEK _____

Goals for the week _____
_____
_____

SUNDAY

Pulse _____ Weight _____ Time _____ AM PM

Weather / Temperature _____ Course _____

Distance _____ Time _____ Pace (mph)_____

COMMENTS _____
_____

MONDAY

Pulse _____ Weight _____ Time _____ AM PM

Weather / Temperature _____ Course _____

Distance _____ Time _____ Pace (mph)_____

COMMENTS _____
_____

TUESDAY

Pulse _____ Weight _____ Time _____ AM PM

Weather / Temperature _____ Course _____

Distance _____ Time _____ Pace (mph)_____

COMMENTS _____
_____

WEDNESDAY

Pulse _____ Weight _____ Time _____ AM PM

Weather / Temperature _____ Course _____

Distance _____ Time _____ Pace (mph)_____

COMMENTS _____
_____

THURSDAY

Pulse _____ Weight _____ Time _____ AM PM

Weather/Temperature _____ Course _____

Distance _____ Time _____ Pace (mph)_____

COMMENTS _____
_____

FRIDAY

Pulse _____ Weight _____ Time _____ AM PM

Weather/Temperature _____ Course _____

Distance _____ Time _____ Pace (mph)_____

COMMENTS _____
_____

SATURDAY

Pulse _____ Weight _____ Time _____ AM PM

Weather/Temperature _____ Course _____

Distance _____ Time _____ Pace (mph)_____

COMMENTS _____
_____

WEEK SUMMARY

Beginning weight _____ Time _____ AM PM

Weight loss (week) _____ (month) _____ (year) _____

Distance _____ (month) _____ (year) _____

Average daily distance this week _____ (this month) _____

COMMENTS _____
_____

10	DISTANCE								10	PACE						
8									8							
6									6							
4									4							
2									2							
MILES	S	M	T	W	T	F	S		MPH	S	M	T	W	T	F	S

WEEK _____ **12**

Goals for the week _____

_____

_____

SUNDAY

Pulse _____ Weight _____ Time _____ AM PM

Weather / Temperature _____ Course _____

Distance _____ Time _____ Pace (mph)_____

COMMENTS _____

_____

MONDAY

Pulse _____ Weight _____ Time _____ AM PM

Weather / Temperature _____ Course _____

Distance _____ Time _____ Pace (mph)_____

COMMENTS _____

_____

TUESDAY

Pulse _____ Weight _____ _____ Time _____ AM PM

Weather / Temperature _____ Course _____

Distance _____ Time _____ Pace (mph)_____

COMMENTS _____

_____

WEDNESDAY

Pulse _____ Weight _____ Time _____ AM PM

Weather / Temperature _____ Course _____

Distance _____ Time _____ Pace (mph)_____

COMMENTS _____

_____

THURSDAY

Pulse _____ Weight _____ Time _____ AM PM

Weather/Temperature _____ Course _____

Distance _____ Time _____ Pace (mph)_____

COMMENTS _____

_____

FRIDAY

Pulse _____ Weight _____ Time _____ AM PM

Weather/Temperature _____ Course _____

Distance _____ Time _____ Pace (mph)_____

COMMENTS _____

_____

SATURDAY

Pulse _____ Weight _____ Time _____ AM PM

Weather/Temperature _____ Course _____

Distance _____ Time _____ Pace (mph)_____

COMMENTS _____

_____

WEEK SUMMARY

Beginning weight _____ Time _____ AM PM

Weight loss (week) _____ (month) _____ (year) _____

Distance _____ (month) _____ (year) _____

Average daily distance this week _____ (this month) _____

COMMENTS _____

_____

DISTANCE

10							
8							
6							
4							
2							
MILES	S	M	T	W	T	F	S

PACE

10							
8							
6							
4							
2							
MPH	S	M	T	W	T	F	S

 WEEK_____ **13**

Goals for the week _____
_____
_____

SUNDAY

Pulse _____ Weight _____ Time _____ AM PM

Weather / Temperature _____ Course _____

Distance _____ Time _____ Pace (mph)_____

COMMENTS _____
_____

MONDAY

Pulse _____ Weight _____ Time _____ AM PM

Weather / Temperature _____ Course _____

Distance _____ Time _____ Pace (mph)_____

COMMENTS _____
_____

TUESDAY

Pulse _____ Weight _____ Time _____ AM PM

Weather / Temperature _____ Course _____

Distance _____ Time _____ Pace (mph)_____

COMMENTS _____
_____

WEDNESDAY

Pulse _____ Weight _____ Time _____ AM PM

Weather / Temperature _____ Course _____

Distance _____ Time _____ Pace (mph)_____

COMMENTS _____
_____

THURSDAY

Pulse _____ Weight _____ Time _____ AM PM

Weather / Temperature _____ Course _____

Distance _____ Time _____ Pace (mph)_____

COMMENTS _____

_____

FRIDAY

Pulse _____ Weight _____ Time _____ AM PM

Weather / Temperature _____ Course _____

Distance _____ Time _____ Pace (mph)_____

COMMENTS _____

_____

SATURDAY

Pulse _____ Weight _____ Time _____ AM PM

Weather / Temperature _____ Course _____

Distance _____ Time _____ Pace (mph)_____

COMMENTS _____

_____

WEEK SUMMARY

Beginning weight _____ Time _____ AM PM

Weight loss (week) _____ (month) _____ (year) _____

Distance _____ (month) _____ (year) _____

Average daily distance this week _____ (this month) _____

COMMENTS _____

_____

DISTANCE

10
8
6
4
2
MILES   S   M   T   W   T   F   S

PACE

10
8
6
4
2
MPH   S   M   T   W   T   F   S

 WEEK _____ **14**

Goals for the week _____
_____
_____

SUNDAY

Pulse _____ Weight _____ Time _____ AM PM

Weather / Temperature _____ Course _____

Distance _____ Time _____ Pace (mph)_____

COMMENTS _____
_____

MONDAY

Pulse _____ Weight _____ Time _____ AM PM

Weather / Temperature _____ Course _____

Distance _____ Time _____ Pace (mph)_____

COMMENTS _____
_____

TUESDAY

Pulse _____ Weight _____ Time _____ AM PM

Weather / Temperature _____ Course _____

Distance _____ Time _____ Pace (mph)_____

COMMENTS _____
_____

WEDNESDAY

Pulse _____ Weight _____ Time _____ AM PM

Weather / Temperature _____ Course _____

Distance _____ Time _____ Pace (mph)_____

COMMENTS _____
_____

THURSDAY

Pulse _____ Weight _____ Time _____ AM PM

Weather / Temperature _____ Course _____

Distance _____ Time _____ Pace (mph)_____

COMMENTS _____

_____

FRIDAY

Pulse _____ Weight _____ Time _____ AM PM

Weather / Temperature _____ Course _____

Distance _____ Time _____ Pace (mph)_____

COMMENTS _____

_____

SATURDAY

Pulse _____ Weight _____ Time _____ AM PM

Weather / Temperature _____ Course _____

Distance _____ Time _____ Pace (mph)_____

COMMENTS _____

_____

WEEK SUMMARY

Beginning weight _____ Time _____ AM PM

Weight loss (week) _____ (month) _____ (year) _____

Distance _____ (month) _____ (year) _____

Average daily distance this week _____ (this month) _____

COMMENTS _____

_____

MILES	DISTANCE	S	M	T	W	T	F	S
10								
8								
6								
4								
2								

MPH	PACE	S	M	T	W	T	F	S
10								
8								
6								
4								
2								

 **WEEK** _____ **15**

Goals for the week _____
_____
_____

SUNDAY

Pulse _____ Weight _____ Time _____ AM PM

Weather / Temperature _____ Course _____

Distance _____ Time _____ Pace (mph)_____

COMMENTS _____
_____

MONDAY

Pulse _____ Weight _____ Time _____ AM PM

Weather / Temperature _____ Course _____

Distance _____ Time _____ Pace (mph)_____

COMMENTS _____
_____

TUESDAY

Pulse _____ Weight _____ Time _____ AM PM

Weather / Temperature _____ Course _____

Distance _____ Time _____ Pace (mph)_____

COMMENTS _____
_____

WEDNESDAY

Pulse _____ Weight _____ Time _____ AM PM

Weather / Temperature _____ Course _____

Distance _____ Time _____ Pace (mph)_____

COMMENTS _____
_____

THURSDAY

Pulse _____ Weight _____ Time _____ AM PM

Weather / Temperature _____ Course _____

Distance _____ Time _____ Pace (mph)_____

COMMENTS _____

_____

FRIDAY

Pulse _____ Weight _____ Time _____ AM PM

Weather / Temperature _____ Course _____

Distance _____ Time _____ Pace (mph)_____

COMMENTS _____

_____

SATURDAY

Pulse _____ Weight _____ Time _____ AM PM

Weather / Temperature _____ Course _____

Distance _____ Time _____ Pace (mph)_____

COMMENTS _____

_____

WEEK SUMMARY

Beginning weight _____ Time _____ AM PM

Weight loss (week) _____ (month) _____ (year) _____

Distance _____ (month) _____ (year) _____

Average daily distance this week _____ (this month) _____

COMMENTS _____

_____

DISTANCE

MILES	10	8	6	4	2							
						S	M	T	W	T	F	S

PACE

MPH	10	8	6	4	2							
						S	M	T	W	T	F	S

WEEK _____ **16**

Goals for the week _____
_____ _____
_____

SUNDAY

Pulse _____ Weight _____ Time _____ AM PM

Weather / Temperature _____ Course _____

Distance _____ Time _____ Pace (mph)_____

COMMENTS _____
_____

MONDAY

Pulse _____ Weight _____ Time _____ AM PM

Weather / Temperature _____ Course _____

Distance _____ Time _____ Pace (mph)_____

COMMENTS _____
_____

TUESDAY

Pulse _____ Weight _____ Time _____ AM PM

Weather / Temperature _____ Course _____

Distance _____ Time _____ Pace (mph)_____

COMMENTS _____
_____

WEDNESDAY

Pulse _____ Weight _____ Time _____ AM PM

Weather / Temperature _____ Course _____

Distance _____ Time _____ Pace (mph)_____

COMMENTS _____
_____

THURSDAY

Pulse _____ Weight _____ Time _____ AM PM

Weather / Temperature _____ Course _____

Distance _____ Time _____ Pace (mph)_____

COMMENTS _____

_____

FRIDAY

Pulse _____ Weight _____ Time _____ AM PM

Weather / Temperature _____ Course _____

Distance _____ Time _____ Pace (mph)_____

COMMENTS _____

_____

SATURDAY

Pulse _____ Weight _____ Time _____ AM PM

Weather / Temperature _____ Course _____

Distance _____ Time _____ Pace (mph)_____

COMMENTS _____

_____

WEEK SUMMARY

Beginning weight _____ Time _____ AM PM

Weight loss (week) _____ (month) _____ (year) _____

Distance _____ (month) _____ (year) _____

Average daily distance this week _____ (this month) _____

COMMENTS _____

_____

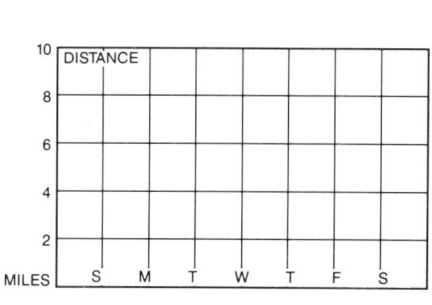

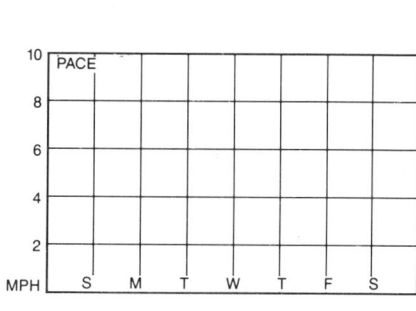

 **WEEK**_____ **17**

Goals for the week _____
_____
_____

SUNDAY

Pulse _____ Weight _____ Time _____ AM PM

Weather / Temperature _____ Course _____

Distance _____ Time _____ Pace (mph)_____

COMMENTS _____
_____

MONDAY

Pulse _____ Weight _____ Time _____ AM PM

Weather / Temperature _____ Course _____

Distance _____ Time _____ Pace (mph)_____

COMMENTS _____
_____

TUESDAY

Pulse _____ Weight _____ Time _____ AM PM

Weather / Temperature _____ Course _____

Distance _____ Time _____ Pace (mph)_____

COMMENTS _____
_____

WEDNESDAY

Pulse _____ Weight _____ Time _____ AM PM

Weather / Temperature _____ Course _____

Distance _____ Time _____ Pace (mph)_____

COMMENTS _____
_____

THURSDAY

Pulse _____ Weight _____ Time _____ AM PM

Weather/Temperature _____ Course _____

Distance _____ Time _____ Pace (mph)_____

COMMENTS_____

_____

FRIDAY

Pulse _____ Weight _____ Time _____ AM PM

Weather/Temperature _____ Course _____

Distance _____ Time _____ Pace (mph)_____

COMMENTS_____

_____

SATURDAY

Pulse _____ Weight _____ Time _____ AM PM

Weather/Temperature _____ Course _____

Distance _____ Time _____ Pace (mph)_____

COMMENTS_____

_____

WEEK SUMMARY

Beginning weight _____ Time _____ AM PM

Weight loss (week) _____ (month) _____ (year) _____

Distance _____ (month) _____ (year) _____

Average daily distance this week _____ (this month) _____

COMMENTS_____

_____

DISTANCE							
10							
8							
6							
4							
2							
MILES	S	M	T	W	T	F	S

PACE							
10							
8							
6							
4							
2							
MPH	S	M	T	W	T	F	S

WEEK _____ **18**

Goals for the week _____
_____
_____

SUNDAY

Pulse _____ Weight _____ Time _____ AM PM

Weather / Temperature _____ Course _____

Distance _____ Time _____ Pace (mph)_____

COMMENTS _____
_____

MONDAY

Pulse _____ Weight _____ Time _____ AM PM

Weather / Temperature _____ Course _____

Distance _____ Time _____ Pace (mph)_____

COMMENTS _____
_____

TUESDAY

Pulse _____ Weight _____ Time _____ AM PM

Weather / Temperature _____ Course _____

Distance _____ Time _____ Pace (mph)_____

COMMENTS _____
_____

WEDNESDAY

Pulse _____ Weight _____ Time _____ AM PM

Weather / Temperature _____ Course _____

Distance _____ Time _____ Pace (mph)_____

COMMENTS _____
_____

THURSDAY

Pulse _____ Weight _____ Time _____ AM PM

Weather / Temperature _____ Course _____

Distance _____ Time _____ Pace (mph)_____

COMMENTS _____

_____

FRIDAY

Pulse _____ Weight _____ Time _____ AM PM

Weather / Temperature _____ Course _____

Distance _____ Time _____ Pace (mph)_____

COMMENTS _____

_____

SATURDAY

Pulse _____ Weight _____ Time _____ AM PM

Weather / Temperature _____ Course _____

Distance _____ Time _____ Pace (mph)_____

COMMENTS _____

_____

WEEK SUMMARY

Beginning weight _____ Time _____ AM PM

Weight loss (week) _____ (month) _____ (year) _____

Distance _____ (month) _____ (year) _____

Average daily distance this week _____ (this month) _____

COMMENTS _____

_____

DISTANCE

MILES	S	M	T	W	T	F	S
10							
8							
6							
4							
2							

PACE

MPH	S	M	T	W	T	F	S
10							
8							
6							
4							
2							

 **WEEK** _____ **19**

Goals for the week _____
_____
_____

SUNDAY

Pulse _____ Weight _____ Time _____ AM PM

Weather / Temperature _____ Course _____

Distance _____ Time _____ Pace (mph)_____

COMMENTS _____
_____

MONDAY

Pulse _____ Weight _____ Time _____ AM PM

Weather / Temperature _____ Course _____

Distance _____ Time _____ Pace (mph)_____

COMMENTS _____
_____

TUESDAY

Pulse _____ Weight _____ Time _____ AM PM

Weather / Temperature _____ Course _____

Distance _____ Time _____ Pace (mph)_____

COMMENTS _____
_____

WEDNESDAY

Pulse _____ Weight _____ Time _____ AM PM

Weather / Temperature _____ Course _____

Distance _____ Time _____ Pace (mph)_____

COMMENTS _____
_____

Pulse _____ Weight _____ Time _____ AM PM

Weather / Temperature _____ Course _____

Distance _____ Time _____ Pace (mph)_____

COMMENTS _____

_____

Pulse _____ Weight _____ Time _____ AM PM

Weather / Temperature _____ Course _____

Distance _____ Time _____ Pace (mph)_____

COMMENTS _____

_____

Pulse _____ Weight _____ Time _____ AM PM

Weather / Temperature _____ Course _____

Distance _____ Time _____ Pace (mph)_____

COMMENTS _____

_____

Beginning weight _____ Time _____ AM PM

Weight loss (week) _____ (month) _____ (year) _____

Distance _____ (month) _____ (year) _____

Average daily distance this week _____ (this month) _____

COMMENTS _____

_____

DISTANCE							
10							
8							
6							
4							
2							
MILES	S	M	T	W	T	F	S

PACE							
10							
8							
6							
4							
2							
MPH	S	M	T	W	T	F	S

WEEK _____ **20**

Goals for the week _____
_____
_____

SUNDAY

Pulse _____ Weight _____ Time _____ AM PM

Weather / Temperature _____ Course _____

Distance _____ Time _____ Pace (mph) _____

COMMENTS _____
_____

MONDAY

Pulse _____ Weight _____ Time _____ AM PM

Weather / Temperature _____ Course _____

Distance _____ Time _____ Pace (mph) _____

COMMENTS _____
_____

TUESDAY

Pulse _____ Weight _____ Time _____ AM PM

Weather / Temperature _____ Course _____

Distance _____ Time _____ Pace (mph) _____

COMMENTS _____
_____

WEDNESDAY

Pulse _____ Weight _____ Time _____ AM PM

Weather / Temperature _____ Course _____

Distance _____ Time _____ Pace (mph) _____

COMMENTS _____
_____

THURSDAY

Pulse _____ Weight _____ Time _____ AM PM

Weather / Temperature _____ Course _____

Distance _____ Time _____ Pace (mph)_____

COMMENTS _____

_____

FRIDAY

Pulse _____ Weight _____ Time _____ AM PM

Weather / Temperature _____ Course _____

Distance _____ Time _____ Pace (mph)_____

COMMENTS _____

_____

SATURDAY

Pulse _____ Weight _____ Time _____ AM PM

Weather / Temperature _____ Course _____

Distance _____ Time _____ Pace (mph)_____

COMMENTS _____

_____

WEEK SUMMARY

Beginning weight _____ Time _____ AM PM

Weight loss (week) _____ (month) _____ (year) _____

Distance _____ (month) _____ (year) _____

Average daily distance this week _____ (this month) _____

COMMENTS _____

_____

```
10 | DISTANCE                          10 | PACE
 8 |                                    8 |
 6 |                                    6 |
 4 |                                    4 |
 2 |                                    2 |
MILES  S   M   T   W   T   F   S       MPH  S   M   T   W   T   F   S
```

 **WEEK** _____ **21**

Goals for the week _____
_____
_____

SUNDAY

Pulse _____ Weight _____ Time _____ AM PM

Weather/Temperature _____ Course _____

Distance _____ Time _____ Pace (mph)_____

COMMENTS _____
_____

MONDAY

Pulse _____ Weight _____ Time _____ AM PM

Weather/Temperature _____ Course _____

Distance _____ Time _____ Pace (mph)_____

COMMENTS _____
_____

TUESDAY

Pulse _____ Weight _____ Time _____ AM PM

Weather/Temperature _____ Course _____

Distance _____ Time _____ Pace (mph)_____

COMMENTS _____
_____

WEDNESDAY

Pulse _____ Weight _____ Time _____ AM PM

Weather/Temperature _____ Course _____

Distance _____ Time _____ Pace (mph)_____

COMMENTS _____
_____

Pulse _____ Weight _____ Time _____ AM PM

Weather / Temperature _____ Course _____

Distance _____ Time _____ Pace (mph)_____

COMMENTS _____

_____

FRIDAY

Pulse _____ Weight _____ Time _____ AM PM

Weather / Temperature _____ Course _____

Distance _____ Time _____ Pace (mph)_____

COMMENTS _____

_____

SATURDAY

Pulse _____ Weight _____ Time _____ AM PM

Weather / Temperature _____ Course _____

Distance _____ Time _____ Pace (mph)_____

COMMENTS _____

_____

WEEK SUMMARY

Beginning weight _____ Time _____ AM PM

Weight loss (week) _____ (month) _____ (year) _____

Distance _____ (month) _____ (year) _____

Average daily distance this week _____ (this month) _____

COMMENTS _____

_____

DISTANCE

10
8
6
4
2
MILES   S   M   T   W   T   F   S

PACE

10
8
6
4
2
MPH   S   M   T   W   T   F   S

 **WEEK**_____ **22**

Goals for the week _____

_____

_____

SUNDAY

Pulse _____ Weight _____ Time _____ AM PM

Weather / Temperature _____ Course _____

Distance _____ Time _____ Pace (mph)_____

COMMENTS _____

_____

MONDAY

Pulse _____ Weight _____ Time _____ AM PM

Weather / Temperature _____ Course _____

Distance _____ Time _____ Pace (mph)_____

COMMENTS _____

_____

TUESDAY

Pulse _____ Weight _____ Time _____ AM PM

Weather / Temperature _____ Course _____

Distance _____ Time _____ Pace (mph)_____

COMMENTS _____

_____

WEDNESDAY

Pulse _____ Weight _____ Time _____ AM PM

Weather / Temperature _____ Course _____

Distance _____ Time _____ Pace (mph)_____

COMMENTS _____

_____

Pulse _____ Weight _____ Time _____ AM PM

Weather / Temperature _____ Course _____

Distance _____ Time _____ Pace (mph)_____

COMMENTS _____

_____

Pulse _____ Weight _____ Time _____ AM PM

Weather / Temperature _____ Course _____

Distance _____ Time _____ Pace (mph)_____

COMMENTS _____

_____

Pulse _____ Weight _____ Time _____ AM PM

Weather / Temperature _____ Course _____

Distance _____ Time _____ Pace (mph)_____

COMMENTS _____

_____

Beginning weight _____ Time _____ AM PM

Weight loss (week) _____ (month) _____ (year) _____

Distance _____ (month) _____ (year) _____

Average daily distance this week _____ (this month) _____

COMMENTS _____

_____

DISTANCE — MILES — S M T W T F S (scale 2–10)

PACE — MPH — S M T W T F S (scale 2–10)

WEEK _____ **23**

Goals for the week _____
_____
_____

SUNDAY

Pulse _____ Weight _____ Time _____ AM PM

Weather/Temperature _____ Course _____

Distance _____ Time _____ Pace (mph)_____

COMMENTS _____
_____

MONDAY

Pulse _____ Weight _____ Time _____ AM PM

Weather/Temperature _____ Course _____

Distance _____ Time _____ Pace (mph)_____

COMMENTS _____
_____

TUESDAY

Pulse _____ Weight _____ Time _____ AM PM

Weather/Temperature _____ Course _____

Distance _____ Time _____ Pace (mph)_____

COMMENTS _____
_____

WEDNESDAY

Pulse _____ Weight _____ Time _____ AM PM

Weather/Temperature _____ Course _____

Distance _____ Time _____ Pace (mph)_____

COMMENTS _____
_____

Pulse _____ Weight _____ Time _____ AM PM

Weather / Temperature _____ Course _____

Distance _____ Time _____ Pace (mph)_____

COMMENTS _____

_____

Pulse _____ Weight _____ Time _____ AM PM

Weather / Temperature _____ Course _____

Distance _____ Time _____ Pace (mph)_____

COMMENTS _____

_____

Pulse _____ Weight _____ Time _____ AM PM

Weather / Temperature _____ Course _____

Distance _____ Time _____ Pace (mph)_____

COMMENTS _____

_____

Beginning weight _____ Time _____ AM PM

Weight loss (week) _____ (month) _____ (year) _____

Distance _____ (month) _____ (year) _____

Average daily distance this week _____ (this month) _____

COMMENTS _____

_____

10 DISTANCE
8
6
4
2
MILES   S   M   T   W   T   F   S

10 PACE
8
6
4
2
MPH   S   M   T   W   T   F   S

WEEK _____ 24

Goals for the week _____
_____
_____

SUNDAY

Pulse _____ Weight _____ Time _____ AM PM

Weather / Temperature _____ Course _____

Distance _____ Time _____ Pace (mph)_____

COMMENTS _____
_____

MONDAY

Pulse _____ Weight _____ Time _____ AM PM

Weather / Temperature _____ Course _____

Distance _____ Time _____ Pace (mph)_____

COMMENTS _____
_____

TUESDAY

Pulse _____ Weight _____ Time _____ AM PM

Weather / Temperature _____ Course _____

Distance _____ Time _____ Pace (mph)_____

COMMENTS _____
_____

WEDNESDAY

Pulse _____ Weight _____ Time _____ AM PM

Weather / Temperature _____ Course _____

Distance _____ Time _____ Pace (mph)_____

COMMENTS _____
_____

THURSDAY

Pulse _____ Weight _____ Time _____ AM PM

Weather / Temperature _____ Course _____

Distance _____ Time _____ Pace (mph)_____

COMMENTS_____

_____

FRIDAY

Pulse _____ Weight _____ Time _____ AM PM

Weather / Temperature _____ Course _____

Distance _____ Time _____ Pace (mph)_____

COMMENTS_____

_____

SATURDAY

Pulse _____ Weight _____ Time _____ AM PM

Weather / Temperature _____ Course _____

Distance _____ Time _____ Pace (mph)_____

COMMENTS_____

_____

WEEK SUMMARY

Beginning weight _____ Time _____ AM PM

Weight loss (week) _____ (month) _____ (year) _____

Distance _____ (month) _____ (year) _____

Average daily distance this week _____ (this month) _____

COMMENTS_____

_____

DISTANCE
10
8
6
4
2
MILES   S   M   T   W   T   F   S

PACE
10
8
6
4
2
MPH   S   M   T   W   T   F   S

Goals for the week _____
_____
_____

SUNDAY

Pulse _____ Weight _____ Time _____ AM PM

Weather / Temperature _____ Course _____

Distance _____ Time _____ Pace (mph)_____

COMMENTS _____
_____

MONDAY

Pulse _____ Weight _____ Time _____ AM PM

Weather / Temperature _____ Course _____

Distance _____ Time _____ Pace (mph)_____

COMMENTS _____
_____

TUESDAY

Pulse _____ Weight _____ Time _____ AM PM

Weather / Temperature _____ Course _____

Distance _____ Time _____ Pace (mph)_____

COMMENTS _____
_____

WEDNESDAY

Pulse _____ Weight _____ Time _____ AM PM

Weather / Temperature _____ Course _____

Distance _____ Time _____ Pace (mph)_____

COMMENTS _____
_____

THURSDAY

Pulse _____ Weight _____ Time _____ AM PM

Weather / Temperature _____ Course _____

Distance _____ Time _____ Pace (mph)_____

COMMENTS _____

_____

FRIDAY

Pulse _____ Weight _____ Time _____ AM PM

Weather / Temperature _____ Course _____

Distance _____ Time _____ Pace (mph)_____

COMMENTS _____

_____

SATURDAY

Pulse _____ Weight _____ Time _____ AM PM

Weather / Temperature _____ Course _____

Distance _____ Time _____ Pace (mph)_____

COMMENTS _____

_____

WEEK SUMMARY

Beginning weight _____ Time _____ AM PM

Weight loss (week) _____ (month) _____ (year) _____

Distance _____ (month) _____ (year) _____

Average daily distance this week _____ (this month) _____

COMMENTS _____

_____

DISTANCE

	S	M	T	W	T	F	S
10							
8							
6							
4							
2							

MILES

PACE

	S	M	T	W	T	F	S
10							
8							
6							
4							
2							

MPH

WEEK _____ **26**

Goals for the week _____
_____
_____

SUNDAY

Pulse _____ Weight _____ Time _____ AM PM

Weather/Temperature _____ Course _____

Distance _____ Time _____ Pace (mph)_____

COMMENTS _____
_____

MONDAY

Pulse _____ Weight _____ Time _____ AM PM

Weather/Temperature _____ Course _____

Distance _____ Time _____ Pace (mph)_____

COMMENTS _____
_____

TUESDAY

Pulse _____ Weight _____ Time _____ AM PM

Weather/Temperature _____ Course _____

Distance _____ Time _____ Pace (mph)_____

COMMENTS _____
_____

WEDNESDAY

Pulse _____ Weight _____ Time _____ AM PM

Weather/Temperature _____ Course _____

Distance _____ Time _____ Pace (mph)_____

COMMENTS _____
_____

THURSDAY

Pulse _____ Weight _____ Time _____ AM PM

Weather / Temperature _____ Course _____

Distance _____ Time _____ Pace (mph)_____

COMMENTS _____

_____

FRIDAY

Pulse _____ Weight _____ Time _____ AM PM

Weather / Temperature _____ Course _____

Distance _____ Time _____ Pace (mph)_____

COMMENTS _____

_____

SATURDAY

Pulse _____ Weight _____ Time _____ AM PM

Weather / Temperature _____ Course _____

Distance _____ Time _____ Pace (mph)_____

COMMENTS _____

_____

WEEK SUMMARY

Beginning weight _____ Time _____ AM PM

Weight loss (week) _____ (month) _____ (year) _____

Distance _____ (month) _____ (year) _____

Average daily distance this week _____ (this month) _____

COMMENTS _____

_____

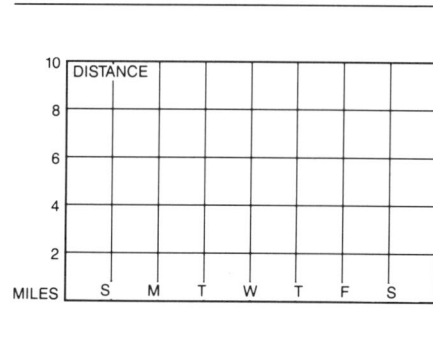

 WEEK _____ **27**

Goals for the week _____
_____
_____

SUNDAY

Pulse _____ Weight _____ Time _____ AM PM

Weather / Temperature _____ Course _____

Distance _____ Time _____ Pace (mph)_____

COMMENTS _____
_____

MONDAY

Pulse _____ Weight _____ Time _____ AM PM

Weather / Temperature _____ Course _____

Distance _____ Time _____ Pace (mph)_____

COMMENTS _____
_____

TUESDAY

Pulse _____ Weight _____ Time _____ AM PM

Weather / Temperature _____ Course _____

Distance _____ Time _____ Pace (mph)_____

COMMENTS _____
_____

WEDNESDAY

Pulse _____ Weight _____ Time _____ AM PM

Weather / Temperature _____ Course _____

Distance _____ Time _____ Pace (mph)_____

COMMENTS _____
_____

Pulse _____ Weight _____ Time _____ AM PM

Weather / Temperature _____ Course _____

Distance _____ Time _____ Pace (mph)_____

COMMENTS _____

_____

Pulse _____ Weight _____ Time _____ AM PM

Weather / Temperature _____ Course _____

Distance _____ Time _____ Pace (mph)_____

COMMENTS _____

_____

Pulse _____ Weight _____ Time _____ AM PM

Weather / Temperature _____ Course _____

Distance _____ Time _____ Pace (mph)_____

COMMENTS _____

_____

Beginning weight _____ Time _____ AM PM

Weight loss (week) _____ (month) _____ (year) _____

Distance _____ (month) _____ (year) _____

Average daily distance this week _____ (this month) _____

COMMENTS _____

_____

DISTANCE

```
10 |
 8 |
 6 |
 4 |
 2 |
MILES  S   M   T   W   T   F   S
```

PACE

```
10 |
 8 |
 6 |
 4 |
 2 |
MPH   S   M   T   W   T   F   S
```

Goals for the week _____

_____

_____

SUNDAY

Pulse _____ Weight _____ Time _____ AM PM

Weather / Temperature _____ Course _____

Distance _____ Time _____ Pace (mph)_____

COMMENTS _____

_____

MONDAY

Pulse _____ Weight _____ Time _____ AM PM

Weather / Temperature _____ Course _____

Distance _____ Time _____ Pace (mph)_____

COMMENTS _____

_____

TUESDAY

Pulse _____ Weight _____ Time _____ AM PM

Weather / Temperature _____ Course _____

Distance _____ Time _____ Pace (mph)_____

COMMENTS _____

_____

WEDNESDAY

Pulse _____ Weight _____ Time _____ AM PM

Weather / Temperature _____ Course _____

Distance _____ Time _____ Pace (mph)_____

COMMENTS _____

_____

Pulse _____ Weight _____ Time _____ AM PM

Weather / Temperature _____ Course _____

Distance _____ Time _____ Pace (mph)_____

COMMENTS _____

_____

Pulse _____ Weight _____ Time _____ AM PM

Weather / Temperature _____ Course _____

Distance _____ Time _____ Pace (mph)_____

COMMENTS _____

_____

Pulse _____ Weight _____ Time _____ AM PM

Weather / Temperature _____ Course _____

Distance _____ Time _____ Pace (mph)_____

COMMENTS _____

_____

Beginning weight _____ Time _____ AM PM

Weight loss (week) _____ (month) _____ (year) _____

Distance _____ (month) _____ (year) _____

Average daily distance this week _____ (this month) _____

COMMENTS _____

_____

DISTANCE

10
8
6
4
2
MILES   S   M   T   W   T   F   S

PACE

10
8
6
4
2
MPH   S   M   T   W   T   F   S

WEEK _____ 29

Goals for the week _____
_____
_____

SUNDAY

Pulse _____ Weight _____ Time _____ AM PM

Weather / Temperature _____ Course _____

Distance _____ Time _____ Pace (mph)_____

COMMENTS _____
_____

MONDAY

Pulse _____ Weight _____ Time _____ AM PM

Weather / Temperature _____ Course _____

Distance _____ Time _____ Pace (mph)_____

COMMENTS _____
_____

TUESDAY

Pulse _____ Weight _____ Time _____ AM PM

Weather / Temperature _____ Course _____

Distance _____ Time _____ Pace (mph)_____

COMMENTS _____
_____

WEDNESDAY

Pulse _____ Weight _____ Time _____ AM PM

Weather / Temperature _____ Course _____

Distance _____ Time _____ Pace (mph)_____

COMMENTS _____
_____

THURSDAY

Pulse _____ Weight _____ Time _____ AM PM

Weather / Temperature _____ Course _____

Distance _____ Time _____ Pace (mph)_____

COMMENTS _____

_____

FRIDAY

Pulse _____ Weight _____ Time _____ AM PM

Weather / Temperature _____ Course _____

Distance _____ Time _____ Pace (mph)_____

COMMENTS _____

_____

SATURDAY

Pulse _____ Weight _____ Time _____ AM PM

Weather / Temperature _____ Course _____

Distance _____ Time _____ Pace (mph)_____

COMMENTS _____

_____

WEEK SUMMARY

Beginning weight _____ Time _____ AM PM

Weight loss (week) _____ (month) _____ (year) _____

Distance _____ (month) _____ (year) _____

Average daily distance this week _____ (this month) _____

COMMENTS _____

_____

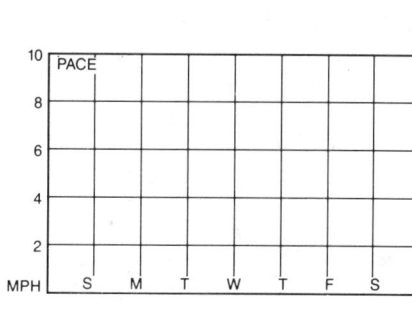

WEEK_____ **30**

Goals for the week _____
_____
_____

SUNDAY

Pulse _____ Weight _____ Time _____ AM PM

Weather / Temperature _____ Course _____

Distance _____ Time _____ Pace (mph)_____

COMMENTS _____
_____

MONDAY

Pulse _____ Weight _____ Time _____ AM PM

Weather / Temperature _____ Course _____

Distance _____ Time _____ Pace (mph)_____

COMMENTS _____
_____

TUESDAY

Pulse _____ Weight _____ Time _____ AM PM

Weather / Temperature _____ Course _____

Distance _____ Time _____ Pace (mph)_____

COMMENTS _____
_____

WEDNESDAY

Pulse _____ Weight _____ Time _____ AM PM

Weather / Temperature _____ Course _____

Distance _____ Time _____ Pace (mph)_____

COMMENTS _____
_____

THURSDAY

Pulse _____ Weight _____ Time _____ AM PM

Weather / Temperature _____ Course _____

Distance _____ Time _____ Pace (mph)_____

COMMENTS _____

_____

FRIDAY

Pulse _____ Weight _____ Time _____ AM PM

Weather / Temperature _____ Course _____

Distance _____ Time _____ Pace (mph)_____

COMMENTS _____

_____

SATURDAY

Pulse _____ Weight _____ Time _____ AM PM

Weather / Temperature _____ Course _____

Distance _____ Time _____ Pace (mph)_____

COMMENTS _____

_____

WEEK SUMMARY

Beginning weight _____ Time _____ AM PM

Weight loss (week) _____ (month) _____ (year) _____

Distance _____ (month) _____ (year) _____

Average daily distance this week _____ (this month) _____

COMMENTS _____

_____

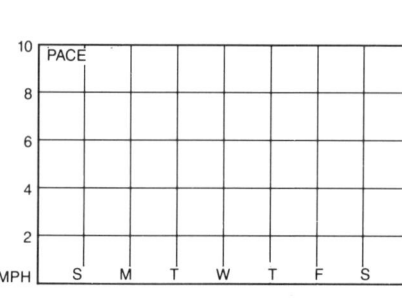

 **WEEK**_____ **31**

Goals for the week _____
_____
_____

SUNDAY

Pulse _____ Weight _____ Time _____ AM PM

Weather / Temperature _____ Course _____

Distance _____ Time _____ Pace (mph)_____

COMMENTS _____
_____

MONDAY

Pulse _____ Weight _____ Time _____ AM PM

Weather / Temperature _____ Course _____

Distance _____ Time _____ Pace (mph)_____

COMMENTS _____
_____

TUESDAY

Pulse _____ Weight _____ Time _____ AM PM

Weather / Temperature _____ Course _____

Distance _____ Time _____ Pace (mph)_____

COMMENTS _____
_____

WEDNESDAY

Pulse _____ Weight _____ Time _____ AM PM

Weather / Temperature _____ Course _____

Distance _____ Time _____ Pace (mph)_____

COMMENTS _____
_____

THURSDAY

Pulse _____ Weight _____ Time _____ AM PM

Weather / Temperature _____ Course _____

Distance _____ Time _____ Pace (mph)_____

COMMENTS _____

_____

FRIDAY

Pulse _____ Weight _____ Time _____ AM PM

Weather / Temperature _____ Course _____

Distance _____ Time _____ Pace (mph)_____

COMMENTS _____

_____

SATURDAY

Pulse _____ Weight _____ Time _____ AM PM

Weather / Temperature _____ Course _____

Distance _____ Time _____ Pace (mph)_____

COMMENTS _____

_____

WEEK SUMMARY

Beginning weight _____ Time _____ AM PM

Weight loss (week) _____ (month) _____ (year) _____

Distance _____ (month) _____ (year) _____

Average daily distance this week _____ (this month) _____

COMMENTS _____

_____

DISTANCE graph: vertical axis MILES, marked 10, 8, 6, 4, 2; horizontal axis days S M T W T F S

PACE graph: vertical axis MPH, marked 10, 8, 6, 4, 2; horizontal axis days S M T W T F S

 WEEK _____ **32**

Goals for the week _____
_____
_____

SUNDAY

Pulse _____ Weight _____ Time _____ AM PM

Weather / Temperature _____ Course _____

Distance _____ Time _____ Pace (mph)_____

COMMENTS _____
_____

MONDAY

Pulse _____ Weight _____ Time _____ AM PM

Weather / Temperature _____ Course _____

Distance _____ Time _____ Pace (mph)_____

COMMENTS _____
_____

TUESDAY

Pulse _____ Weight _____ Time _____ AM PM

Weather / Temperature _____ Course _____

Distance _____ Time _____ Pace (mph)_____

COMMENTS _____
_____

WEDNESDAY

Pulse _____ Weight _____ Time _____ AM PM

Weather / Temperature _____ Course _____

Distance _____ Time _____ Pace (mph)_____

COMMENTS _____
_____

THURSDAY

Pulse _____ Weight _____ Time _____ AM PM

Weather/Temperature _____ Course _____

Distance _____ Time _____ Pace (mph)_____

COMMENTS _____

_____

FRIDAY

Pulse _____ Weight _____ Time _____ AM PM

Weather/Temperature _____ Course _____

Distance _____ Time _____ Pace (mph)_____

COMMENTS _____

_____

SATURDAY

Pulse _____ Weight _____ Time _____ AM PM

Weather/Temperature _____ Course _____

Distance _____ Time _____ Pace (mph)_____

COMMENTS _____

_____

WEEK SUMMARY

Beginning weight _____ Time _____ AM PM

Weight loss (week) _____ (month) _____ (year) _____

Distance _____ (month) _____ (year) _____

Average daily distance this week _____ (this month) _____

COMMENTS _____

_____

DISTANCE

MILES	S	M	T	W	T	F	S
10							
8							
6							
4							
2							

PACE

MPH	S	M	T	W	T	F	S
10							
8							
6							
4							
2							

WEEK_____ **33**

Goals for the week _____
_____
_____

SUNDAY

Pulse _____ Weight _____ Time _____ AM PM

Weather / Temperature _____ Course _____

Distance _____ Time _____ Pace (mph)_____

COMMENTS _____
_____

MONDAY

Pulse _____ Weight _____ Time _____ AM PM

Weather / Temperature _____ Course _____

Distance _____ Time _____ Pace (mph)_____

COMMENTS _____
_____

TUESDAY

Pulse _____ Weight _____ Time _____ AM PM

Weather / Temperature _____ Course _____

Distance _____ Time _____ Pace (mph)_____

COMMENTS _____
_____

WEDNESDAY

Pulse _____ Weight _____ Time _____ AM PM

Weather / Temperature _____ Course _____

Distance _____ Time _____ Pace (mph)_____

COMMENTS _____
_____

THURSDAY

Pulse _____ Weight _____ Time _____ AM PM

Weather / Temperature _____ Course _____

Distance _____ Time _____ Pace (mph)_____

COMMENTS _____

_____

FRIDAY

Pulse _____ Weight _____ Time _____ AM PM

Weather / Temperature _____ Course _____

Distance _____ Time _____ Pace (mph)_____

COMMENTS _____

_____

SATURDAY

Pulse _____ Weight _____ Time _____ AM PM

Weather / Temperature _____ Course _____

Distance _____ Time _____ Pace (mph)_____

COMMENTS _____

_____

WEEK SUMMARY

Beginning weight _____ Time _____ AM PM

Weight loss (week) _____ (month) _____ (year) _____

Distance _____ (month) _____ (year) _____

Average daily distance this week _____ (this month) _____

COMMENTS _____

_____

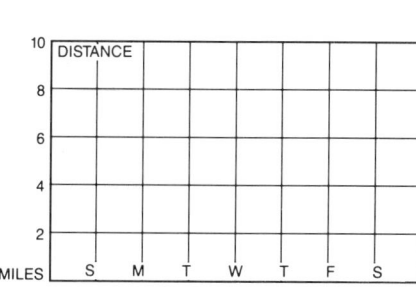

WEEK _____ **34**

Goals for the week _____
_____
_____

SUNDAY

Pulse _____ Weight _____ Time _____ AM PM

Weather/Temperature _____ Course _____

Distance _____ Time _____ Pace (mph)_____

COMMENTS _____
_____

MONDAY

Pulse _____ Weight _____ Time _____ AM PM

Weather/Temperature _____ Course _____

Distance _____ Time _____ Pace (mph)_____

COMMENTS _____
_____

TUESDAY

Pulse _____ Weight _____ Time _____ AM PM

Weather/Temperature _____ Course _____

Distance _____ Time _____ Pace (mph)_____

COMMENTS _____
_____

WEDNESDAY

Pulse _____ Weight _____ Time _____ AM PM

Weather/Temperature _____ Course _____

Distance _____ Time _____ Pace (mph)_____

COMMENTS _____
_____

THURSDAY

Pulse _____ Weight _____ Time _____ AM PM

Weather / Temperature _____ Course _____

Distance _____ Time _____ Pace (mph)_____

COMMENTS _____

_____

FRIDAY

Pulse _____ Weight _____ Time _____ AM PM

Weather / Temperature _____ Course _____

Distance _____ Time _____ Pace (mph)_____

COMMENTS _____

_____

SATURDAY

Pulse _____ Weight _____ Time _____ AM PM

Weather / Temperature _____ Course _____

Distance _____ Time _____ Pace (mph)_____

COMMENTS _____

_____

WEEK SUMMARY

Beginning weight _____ Time _____ AM PM

Weight loss (week) _____ (month) _____ (year) _____

Distance _____ (month) _____ (year) _____

Average daily distance this week _____ (this month) _____

COMMENTS _____

_____

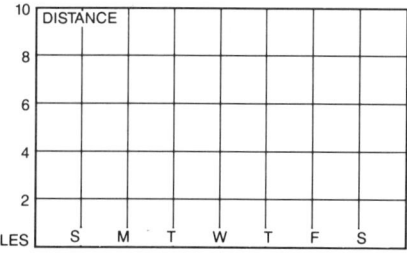

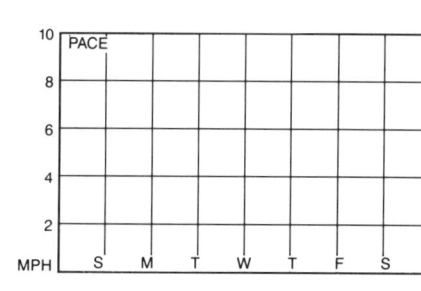

 **WEEK** _____ **35**

Goals for the week _____
_____
_____

SUNDAY

Pulse _____ Weight _____ Time _____ AM PM

Weather / Temperature _____ Course _____

Distance _____ Time _____ Pace (mph)_____

COMMENTS _____
_____

MONDAY

Pulse _____ Weight _____ Time _____ AM PM

Weather / Temperature _____ Course _____

Distance _____ Time _____ Pace (mph)_____

COMMENTS _____
_____

TUESDAY

Pulse _____ Weight _____ Time _____ AM PM

Weather / Temperature _____ Course _____

Distance _____ Time _____ Pace (mph)_____

COMMENTS _____
_____

WEDNESDAY

Pulse _____ Weight _____ Time _____ AM PM

Weather / Temperature _____ Course _____

Distance _____ Time _____ Pace (mph)_____

COMMENTS _____
_____

Pulse _____ Weight _____ Time _____ AM PM

Weather / Temperature _____ Course _____

Distance _____ Time _____ Pace (mph)_____

COMMENTS _____

_____

Pulse _____ Weight _____ Time _____ AM PM

Weather / Temperature _____ Course _____

Distance _____ Time _____ Pace (mph)_____

COMMENTS _____

_____

Pulse _____ Weight _____ Time _____ AM PM

Weather / Temperature _____ Course _____

Distance _____ Time _____ Pace (mph)_____

COMMENTS _____

_____

WEEK SUMMARY

Beginning weight _____ Time _____ AM PM

Weight loss (week) _____ (month) _____ (year) _____

Distance _____ (month) _____ (year) _____

Average daily distance this week _____ (this month) _____

COMMENTS _____

_____

 **WEEK** _____ **36**

Goals for the week _____
_____
_____

SUNDAY

Pulse _____ Weight _____ Time _____ AM PM

Weather / Temperature _____ Course _____

Distance _____ Time _____ Pace (mph)_____

COMMENTS _____
_____

MONDAY

Pulse _____ Weight _____ Time _____ AM PM

Weather / Temperature _____ Course _____

Distance _____ Time _____ Pace (mph)_____

COMMENTS _____
_____

TUESDAY

Pulse _____ Weight _____ Time _____ AM PM

Weather / Temperature _____ Course _____

Distance _____ Time _____ Pace (mph)_____

COMMENTS _____
_____

WEDNESDAY

Pulse _____ Weight _____ Time _____ AM PM

Weather / Temperature _____ Course _____

Distance _____ Time _____ Pace (mph)_____

COMMENTS _____
_____

THURSDAY

Pulse _____ Weight _____ Time _____ AM PM

Weather / Temperature _____ Course _____

Distance _____ Time _____ Pace (mph)_____

COMMENTS _____

_____

FRIDAY

Pulse _____ Weight _____ Time _____ AM PM

Weather / Temperature _____ Course _____

Distance _____ Time _____ Pace (mph)_____

COMMENTS _____

_____

SATURDAY

Pulse _____ Weight _____ Time _____ AM PM

Weather / Temperature _____ Course _____

Distance _____ Time _____ Pace (mph)_____

COMMENTS _____

_____

Beginning weight _____ Time _____ AM PM

Weight loss (week) _____ (month) _____ (year) _____

Distance _____ (month) _____ (year) _____

Average daily distance this week _____ (this month) _____

COMMENTS _____

_____

DISTANCE

10
8
6
4
2
MILES   S   M   T   W   T   F   S

PACE

10
8
6
4
2
MPH   S   M   T   W   T   F   S

 **WEEK**_____ **37**

Goals for the week _____
_____
_____

SUNDAY

Pulse _____ Weight _____ Time _____ AM PM

Weather / Temperature _____ Course _____

Distance _____ Time _____ Pace (mph)_____

COMMENTS _____
_____

MONDAY

Pulse _____ Weight _____ Time _____ AM PM

Weather / Temperature _____ Course _____

Distance _____ Time _____ Pace (mph)_____

COMMENTS _____
_____

TUESDAY

Pulse _____ Weight _____ Time _____ AM PM

Weather / Temperature _____ Course _____

Distance _____ Time _____ Pace (mph)_____

COMMENTS _____
_____

WEDNESDAY

Pulse _____ Weight _____ Time _____ AM PM

Weather / Temperature _____ Course _____

Distance _____ Time _____ Pace (mph)_____

COMMENTS _____
_____

Pulse _____ Weight _____ Time _____ AM PM

Weather / Temperature _____ Course _____

Distance _____ Time _____ Pace (mph)_____

COMMENTS _____

_____

Pulse _____ Weight _____ Time _____ AM PM

Weather / Temperature _____ Course _____

Distance _____ Time _____ Pace (mph)_____

COMMENTS _____

_____

Pulse _____ Weight _____ Time _____ AM PM

Weather / Temperature _____ Course _____

Distance _____ Time _____ Pace (mph)_____

COMMENTS _____

_____

Beginning weight _____ Time _____ AM PM

Weight loss (week) _____ (month) _____ (year) _____

Distance _____ (month) _____ (year) _____

Average daily distance this week _____ (this month) _____

COMMENTS _____

_____

DISTANCE

10
8
6
4
2
MILES S M T W T F S

PACE

10
8
6
4
2
MPH S M T W T F S

WEEK _____ **38**

Goals for the week _____
_____
_____

SUNDAY

Pulse _____ Weight _____ Time _____ AM PM

Weather / Temperature _____ Course _____

Distance _____ Time _____ Pace (mph)_____

COMMENTS _____
_____

MONDAY

Pulse _____ Weight _____ Time _____ AM PM

Weather / Temperature _____ Course _____

Distance _____ Time _____ Pace (mph)_____

COMMENTS _____
_____

TUESDAY

Pulse _____ Weight _____ Time _____ AM PM

Weather / Temperature _____ Course _____

Distance _____ Time _____ Pace (mph)_____

COMMENTS _____
_____

WEDNESDAY

Pulse _____ Weight _____ Time _____ AM PM

Weather / Temperature _____ Course _____

Distance _____ Time _____ Pace (mph)_____

COMMENTS _____
_____

Pulse _____ Weight _____ Time _____ AM PM

Weather / Temperature _____ Course _____

Distance _____ Time _____ Pace (mph)_____

COMMENTS _____

_____

Pulse _____ Weight _____ Time _____ AM PM

Weather / Temperature _____ Course _____

Distance _____ Time _____ Pace (mph)_____

COMMENTS _____

_____

Pulse _____ Weight _____ Time _____ AM PM

Weather / Temperature _____ Course _____

Distance _____ Time _____ Pace (mph)_____

COMMENTS _____

_____

Beginning weight _____ Time _____ AM PM

Weight loss (week) _____ (month) _____ (year) _____

Distance _____ (month) _____ (year) _____

Average daily distance this week _____ (this month) _____

COMMENTS _____

_____

DISTANCE

```
10 | DISTANCE
 8 |
 6 |
 4 |
 2 |
MILES  S  M  T  W  T  F  S
```

PACE

```
10 | PACE
 8 |
 6 |
 4 |
 2 |
MPH  S  M  T  W  T  F  S
```

WEEK _____

Goals for the week _____

_____

_____

SUNDAY

Pulse _____ Weight _____ Time _____ AM PM

Weather / Temperature _____ Course _____

Distance _____ Time _____ Pace (mph)_____

COMMENTS _____

_____

MONDAY

Pulse _____ Weight _____ Time _____ AM PM

Weather / Temperature _____ Course _____

Distance _____ Time _____ Pace (mph)_____

COMMENTS _____

_____

TUESDAY

Pulse _____ Weight _____ Time _____ AM PM

Weather / Temperature _____ Course _____

Distance _____ Time _____ Pace (mph)_____

COMMENTS _____

_____

WEDNESDAY

Pulse _____ Weight _____ Time _____ AM PM

Weather / Temperature _____ Course _____

Distance _____ Time _____ Pace (mph)_____

COMMENTS _____

_____

Pulse _____ Weight _____ Time _____ AM PM

Weather / Temperature _____ Course _____

Distance _____ Time _____ Pace (mph)_____

COMMENTS _____

_____

Pulse _____ Weight _____ Time _____ AM PM

Weather / Temperature _____ Course _____

Distance _____ Time _____ Pace (mph)_____

COMMENTS _____

_____

Pulse _____ Weight _____ Time _____ AM PM

Weather / Temperature _____ Course _____

Distance _____ Time _____ Pace (mph)_____

COMMENTS _____

_____

Beginning weight _____ Time _____ AM PM

Weight loss (week) _____ (month) _____ (year) _____

Distance _____ (month) _____ (year) _____

Average daily distance this week _____ (this month) _____

COMMENTS _____

_____

DISTANCE graph (MILES): y-axis 10, 8, 6, 4, 2; x-axis S M T W T F S

PACE graph (MPH): y-axis 10, 8, 6, 4, 2; x-axis S M T W T F S

 WEEK _____

Goals for the week _____

_____

_____

SUNDAY

Pulse _____ Weight _____ Time _____ AM PM

Weather / Temperature _____ Course _____

Distance _____ Time _____ Pace (mph)_____

COMMENTS _____

_____

MONDAY

Pulse _____ Weight _____ Time _____ AM PM

Weather / Temperature _____ Course _____

Distance _____ Time _____ Pace (mph)_____

COMMENTS _____

_____

TUESDAY

Pulse _____ Weight _____ Time _____ AM PM

Weather / Temperature _____ Course _____

Distance _____ Time _____ Pace (mph)_____

COMMENTS _____

_____

WEDNESDAY

Pulse _____ Weight _____ Time _____ AM PM

Weather / Temperature _____ Course _____

Distance _____ Time _____ Pace (mph)_____

COMMENTS _____

_____

THURSDAY

Pulse _____ Weight _____ Time _____ AM PM

Weather / Temperature _____ Course _____

Distance _____ Time _____ Pace (mph)_____

COMMENTS _____

_____

FRIDAY

Pulse _____ Weight _____ Time _____ AM PM

Weather / Temperature _____ Course _____

Distance _____ Time _____ Pace (mph)_____

COMMENTS _____

_____

SATURDAY

Pulse _____ Weight _____ Time _____ AM PM

Weather / Temperature _____ Course _____

Distance _____ Time _____ Pace (mph)_____

COMMENTS _____

_____

WEEK SUMMARY

Beginning weight _____ Time _____ AM PM

Weight loss (week) _____ (month) _____ (year) _____

Distance _____ (month) _____ (year) _____

Average daily distance this week _____ (this month) _____

COMMENTS _____

_____

DISTANCE
```
10
 8
 6
 4
 2
MILES   S   M   T   W   T   F   S
```

PACE
```
10
 8
 6
 4
 2
MPH    S   M   T   W   T   F   S
```

 **WEEK** _____ **41**

Goals for the week _____
_____
_____

SUNDAY

Pulse _____ Weight _____ Time _____ AM PM

Weather / Temperature _____ Course _____

Distance _____ Time _____ Pace (mph)_____

COMMENTS _____
_____

MONDAY

Pulse _____ Weight _____ Time _____ AM PM

Weather / Temperature _____ Course _____

Distance _____ Time _____ Pace (mph)_____

COMMENTS _____
_____

TUESDAY

Pulse _____ Weight _____ Time _____ AM PM

Weather / Temperature _____ Course _____

Distance _____ Time _____ Pace (mph)_____

COMMENTS _____
_____

WEDNESDAY

Pulse _____ Weight _____ Time _____ AM PM

Weather / Temperature _____ Course _____

Distance _____ Time _____ Pace (mph)_____

COMMENTS _____
_____

Pulse _____ Weight _____ Time _____ AM PM

Weather / Temperature _____ Course _____

Distance _____ Time _____ Pace (mph)_____

COMMENTS _____

_____

Pulse _____ Weight _____ Time _____ AM PM

Weather / Temperature _____ Course _____

Distance _____ Time _____ Pace (mph)_____

COMMENTS _____

_____

Pulse _____ Weight _____ Time _____ AM PM

Weather / Temperature _____ Course _____

Distance _____ Time _____ Pace (mph)_____

COMMENTS _____

_____

Beginning weight _____ Time _____ AM PM

Weight loss (week) _____ (month) _____ (year) _____

Distance _____ (month) _____ (year) _____

Average daily distance this week _____ (this month) _____

COMMENTS _____

_____

DISTANCE
10
8
6
4
2
MILES S M T W T F S

PACE
10
8
6
4
2
MPH S M T W T F S

 WEEK _____

Goals for the week _____

_____

_____

SUNDAY

Pulse _____ Weight _____ Time _____ AM PM

Weather / Temperature _____ Course _____

Distance _____ Time _____ Pace (mph)_____

COMMENTS _____

_____

MONDAY

Pulse _____ Weight _____ Time _____ AM PM

Weather / Temperature _____ Course _____

Distance _____ Time _____ Pace (mph)_____

COMMENTS _____

_____

TUESDAY

Pulse _____ Weight _____ Time _____ AM PM

Weather / Temperature _____ Course _____

Distance _____ Time _____ Pace (mph)_____

COMMENTS _____

_____

WEDNESDAY

Pulse _____ Weight _____ Time _____ AM PM

Weather / Temperature _____ Course _____

Distance _____ Time _____ Pace (mph)_____

COMMENTS _____

_____

Pulse _____ Weight _____ Time _____ AM PM

Weather / Temperature _____ Course _____

Distance _____ Time _____ Pace (mph)_____

COMMENTS _____

_____

Pulse _____ Weight _____ Time _____ AM PM

Weather / Temperature _____ Course _____

Distance _____ Time _____ Pace (mph)_____

COMMENTS _____

_____

Pulse _____ Weight _____ Time _____ AM PM

Weather / Temperature _____ Course _____

Distance _____ Time _____ Pace (mph)_____

COMMENTS _____

_____

Beginning weight _____ Time _____ AM PM

Weight loss (week) _____ (month) _____ (year) _____

Distance _____ (month) _____ (year) _____

Average daily distance this week _____ (this month) _____

COMMENTS _____

_____

DISTANCE
10
8
6
4
2
MILES | S M T W T F S

PACE
10
8
6
4
2
MPH | S M T W T F S

WEEK _____

43

Goals for the week _____
_____
_____

SUNDAY

Pulse _____ Weight _____ Time _____ AM PM

Weather / Temperature _____ Course _____

Distance _____ Time _____ Pace (mph)_____

COMMENTS _____
_____

MONDAY

Pulse _____ Weight _____ Time _____ AM PM

Weather / Temperature _____ Course _____

Distance _____ Time _____ Pace (mph)_____

COMMENTS _____
_____

TUESDAY

Pulse _____ Weight _____ Time _____ AM PM

Weather / Temperature _____ Course _____

Distance _____ Time _____ Pace (mph)_____

COMMENTS _____
_____

WEDNESDAY

Pulse _____ Weight _____ Time _____ AM PM

Weather / Temperature _____ Course _____

Distance _____ Time _____ Pace (mph)_____

COMMENTS _____
_____

Pulse _____ Weight _____ Time _____ AM PM

Weather / Temperature _____ Course _____

Distance _____ Time _____ Pace (mph)_____

COMMENTS _____

_____

Pulse _____ Weight _____ Time _____ AM PM

Weather / Temperature _____ Course _____

Distance _____ Time _____ Pace (mph)_____

COMMENTS _____

_____

Pulse _____ Weight _____ Time _____ AM PM

Weather / Temperature _____ Course _____

Distance _____ Time _____ Pace (mph)_____

COMMENTS _____

_____

Beginning weight _____ Time _____ AM PM

Weight loss (week) _____ (month) _____ (year) _____

Distance _____ (month) _____ (year) _____

Average daily distance this week _____ (this month) _____

COMMENTS _____

_____

10 DISTANCE								10 PACE						
8								8						
6								6						
4								4						
2								2						
MILES	S	M	T	W	T	F	S	MPH	S	M	T	W	T	F	S

WEEK _____

44

Goals for the week _____

_____

_____

SUNDAY

Pulse _____ Weight _____ Time _____ AM PM

Weather / Temperature _____ Course _____

Distance _____ Time _____ Pace (mph)_____

COMMENTS _____

_____

MONDAY

Pulse _____ Weight _____ Time _____ AM PM

Weather / Temperature _____ Course _____

Distance _____ Time _____ Pace (mph)_____

COMMENTS _____

_____

TUESDAY

Pulse _____ Weight _____ Time _____ AM PM

Weather / Temperature _____ Course _____

Distance _____ Time _____ Pace (mph)_____

COMMENTS _____

_____

WEDNESDAY

Pulse _____ Weight _____ Time _____ AM PM

Weather / Temperature _____ Course _____

Distance _____ Time _____ Pace (mph)_____

COMMENTS _____

_____

THURSDAY

Pulse _____ Weight _____ Time _____ AM PM

Weather / Temperature _____ Course _____

Distance _____ Time _____ Pace (mph)_____

COMMENTS _____

_____

FRIDAY

Pulse _____ Weight _____ Time _____ AM PM

Weather / Temperature _____ Course _____

Distance _____ Time _____ Pace (mph)_____

COMMENTS _____

_____

SATURDAY

Pulse _____ Weight _____ Time _____ AM PM

Weather / Temperature _____ Course _____

Distance _____ Time _____ Pace (mph)_____

COMMENTS _____

_____

WEEK SUMMARY

Beginning weight _____ Time _____ AM PM

Weight loss (week) _____ (month) _____ (year) _____

Distance _____ (month) _____ (year) _____

Average daily distance this week _____ (this month) _____

COMMENTS _____

_____

```
10 | DISTANCE                        10 | PACE
 8 |                                  8 |
 6 |                                  6 |
 4 |                                  4 |
 2 |                                  2 |
MILES  S   M   T   W   T   F   S    MPH  S   M   T   W   T   F   S
```

 **WEEK**_____

Goals for the week _____
_____
_____

SUNDAY

Pulse _____ Weight _____ Time _____ AM PM

Weather / Temperature _____ Course _____

Distance _____ Time _____ Pace (mph)_____

COMMENTS _____
_____

MONDAY

Pulse _____ Weight _____ Time _____ AM PM

Weather / Temperature _____ Course _____

Distance _____ Time _____ Pace (mph)_____

COMMENTS _____
_____

TUESDAY

Pulse _____ Weight _____ Time _____ AM PM

Weather / Temperature _____ Course _____

Distance _____ Time _____ Pace (mph)_____

COMMENTS _____
_____

WEDNESDAY

Pulse _____ Weight _____ Time _____ AM PM

Weather / Temperature _____ Course _____

Distance _____ Time _____ Pace (mph)_____

COMMENTS _____
_____

THURSDAY

Pulse _____ Weight _____ Time _____ AM PM

Weather / Temperature _____ Course _____

Distance _____ Time _____ Pace (mph)_____

COMMENTS _____

_____

FRIDAY

Pulse _____ Weight _____ Time _____ AM PM

Weather / Temperature _____ Course _____

Distance _____ Time _____ Pace (mph)_____

COMMENTS _____

_____

SATURDAY

Pulse _____ Weight _____ Time _____ AM PM

Weather / Temperature _____ Course _____

Distance _____ Time _____ Pace (mph)_____

COMMENTS _____

_____

WEEK SUMMARY

Beginning weight _____ Time _____ AM PM

Weight loss (week) _____ (month) _____ (year) _____

Distance _____ (month) _____ (year) _____

Average daily distance this week _____ (this month) _____

COMMENTS _____

_____

10	DISTANCE						
8							
6							
4							
2							
MILES	S	M	T	W	T	F	S

10	PACE						
8							
6							
4							
2							
MPH	S	M	T	W	T	F	S

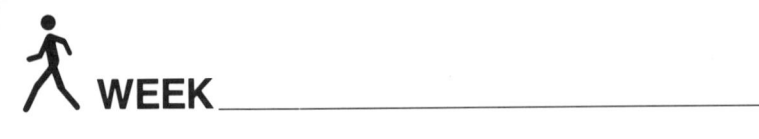

WEEK _____ 46

Goals for the week _____
_____
_____

SUNDAY

Pulse _____ Weight _____ Time _____ AM PM

Weather / Temperature _____ Course _____

Distance _____ Time _____ Pace (mph)_____

COMMENTS _____
_____

MONDAY

Pulse _____ Weight _____ Time _____ AM PM

Weather / Temperature _____ Course _____

Distance _____ Time _____ Pace (mph)_____

COMMENTS _____
_____

TUESDAY

Pulse _____ Weight _____ Time _____ AM PM

Weather / Temperature _____ Course _____

Distance _____ Time _____ Pace (mph)_____

COMMENTS _____
_____

WEDNESDAY

Pulse _____ Weight _____ Time _____ AM PM

Weather / Temperature _____ Course _____

Distance _____ Time _____ Pace (mph)_____

COMMENTS _____
_____

THURSDAY

Pulse _____ Weight _____ Time _____ AM PM

Weather / Temperature _____ Course _____

Distance _____ Time _____ Pace (mph)_____

COMMENTS _____

_____

FRIDAY

Pulse _____ Weight _____ Time _____ AM PM

Weather / Temperature _____ Course _____

Distance _____ Time _____ Pace (mph)_____

COMMENTS _____

_____

SATURDAY

Pulse _____ Weight _____ Time _____ AM PM

Weather / Temperature _____ Course _____

Distance _____ Time _____ Pace (mph)_____

COMMENTS _____

_____

WEEK SUMMARY

Beginning weight _____ Time _____ AM PM

Weight loss (week) _____ (month) _____ (year) _____

Distance _____ (month) _____ (year) _____

Average daily distance this week _____ (this month) _____

COMMENTS _____

_____

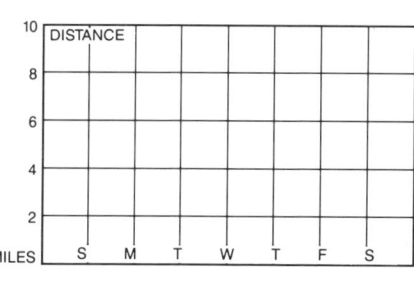

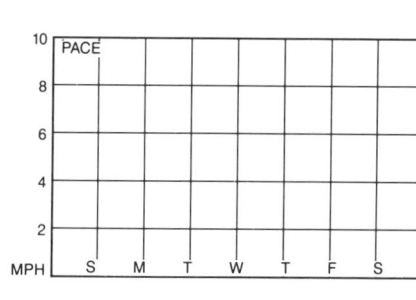

WEEK _____

Goals for the week _____
_____
_____

SUNDAY

Pulse _____ Weight _____ Time _____ AM PM

Weather / Temperature _____ Course _____

Distance _____ Time _____ Pace (mph)_____

COMMENTS _____
_____

MONDAY

Pulse _____ Weight _____ Time _____ AM PM

Weather / Temperature _____ Course _____

Distance _____ Time _____ Pace (mph)_____

COMMENTS _____
_____

TUESDAY

Pulse _____ Weight _____ Time _____ AM PM

Weather / Temperature _____ Course _____

Distance _____ Time _____ Pace (mph)_____

COMMENTS _____
_____

WEDNESDAY

Pulse _____ Weight _____ Time _____ AM PM

Weather / Temperature _____ Course _____

Distance _____ Time _____ Pace (mph)_____

COMMENTS _____
_____

THURSDAY

Pulse _____ Weight _____ Time _____ AM PM

Weather / Temperature _____ Course _____

Distance _____ Time _____ Pace (mph)_____

COMMENTS _____

_____

FRIDAY

Pulse _____ Weight _____ Time _____ AM PM

Weather / Temperature _____ Course _____

Distance _____ Time _____ Pace (mph)_____

COMMENTS _____

_____

SATURDAY

Pulse _____ Weight _____ Time _____ AM PM

Weather / Temperature _____ Course _____

Distance _____ Time _____ Pace (mph)_____

COMMENTS _____

_____

WEEK SUMMARY

Beginning weight _____ Time _____ AM PM

Weight loss (week) _____ (month) _____ (year) _____

Distance _____ (month) _____ (year) _____

Average daily distance this week _____ (this month) _____

COMMENTS _____

_____

DISTANCE

MILES	S	M	T	W	T	F	S
10							
8							
6							
4							
2							

PACE

MPH	S	M	T	W	T	F	S
10							
8							
6							
4							
2							

Goals for the week _____

_____

_____

SUNDAY

Pulse _____ Weight _____ Time _____ AM PM

Weather / Temperature _____ Course _____

Distance _____ Time _____ Pace (mph)_____

COMMENTS _____

_____

MONDAY

Pulse _____ Weight _____ Time _____ AM PM

Weather / Temperature _____ Course _____

Distance _____ Time _____ Pace (mph)_____

COMMENTS _____

_____

TUESDAY

Pulse _____ Weight _____ Time _____ AM PM

Weather / Temperature _____ Course _____

Distance _____ Time _____ Pace (mph)_____

COMMENTS _____

_____

WEDNESDAY

Pulse _____ Weight _____ Time _____ AM PM

Weather / Temperature _____ Course _____

Distance _____ Time _____ Pace (mph)_____

COMMENTS _____

_____

THURSDAY

Pulse _____ Weight _____ Time _____ AM PM

Weather / Temperature _____ Course _____

Distance _____ Time _____ Pace (mph)_____

COMMENTS _____

_____

FRIDAY

Pulse _____ Weight _____ Time _____ AM PM

Weather / Temperature _____ Course _____

Distance _____ Time _____ Pace (mph)_____

COMMENTS _____

_____

SATURDAY

Pulse _____ Weight _____ Time _____ AM PM

Weather / Temperature _____ Course _____

Distance _____ Time _____ Pace (mph)_____

COMMENTS _____

_____

WEEK SUMMARY

Beginning weight _____ Time _____ AM PM

Weight loss (week) _____ (month) _____ (year) _____

Distance _____ (month) _____ (year) _____

Average daily distance this week _____ (this month) _____

COMMENTS _____

_____

DISTANCE

```
10 │ DISTANCE │ │ │ │ │ │
 8 │        │ │ │ │ │ │
 6 │        │ │ │ │ │ │
 4 │        │ │ │ │ │ │
 2 │        │ │ │ │ │ │
MILES  S   M   T   W   T   F   S
```

```
10 │ PACE │ │ │ │ │ │
 8 │      │ │ │ │ │ │
 6 │      │ │ │ │ │ │
 4 │      │ │ │ │ │ │
 2 │      │ │ │ │ │ │
MPH   S   M   T   W   T   F   S
```

 **WEEK** _____ **49**

Goals for the week _____
_____
_____

SUNDAY

Pulse _____ Weight _____ Time _____ AM PM

Weather / Temperature _____ Course _____

Distance _____ Time _____ Pace (mph)_____

COMMENTS _____
_____

MONDAY

Pulse _____ Weight _____ Time _____ AM PM

Weather / Temperature _____ Course _____

Distance _____ Time _____ Pace (mph)_____

COMMENTS _____
_____

TUESDAY

Pulse _____ Weight _____ Time _____ AM PM

Weather / Temperature _____ Course _____

Distance _____ Time _____ Pace (mph)_____

COMMENTS _____
_____

WEDNESDAY

Pulse _____ Weight _____ Time _____ AM PM

Weather / Temperature _____ Course _____

Distance _____ Time _____ Pace (mph)_____

COMMENTS _____
_____

Pulse _____ Weight _____ Time _____ AM PM

Weather / Temperature _____ Course _____

Distance _____ Time _____ Pace (mph)_____

COMMENTS _____

_____

Pulse _____ Weight _____ Time _____ AM PM

Weather / Temperature _____ Course _____

Distance _____ Time _____ Pace (mph)_____

COMMENTS _____

_____

Pulse _____ Weight _____ Time _____ AM PM

Weather / Temperature _____ Course _____

Distance _____ Time _____ Pace (mph)_____

COMMENTS _____

_____

Beginning weight _____ Time _____ AM PM

Weight loss (week) _____ (month) _____ (year) _____

Distance _____ (month) _____ (year) _____

Average daily distance this week _____ (this month) _____

COMMENTS _____

_____

DISTANCE

10
8
6
4
2
MILES   S   M   T   W   T   F   S

PACE

10
8
6
4
2
MPH   S   M   T   W   T   F   S

 WEEK _____ **50**

Goals for the week _____
_____
_____

SUNDAY

Pulse _____ Weight _____ Time _____ AM PM

Weather / Temperature _____ Course _____

Distance _____ Time _____ Pace (mph)_____

COMMENTS _____
_____

MONDAY

Pulse _____ Weight _____ Time _____ AM PM

Weather / Temperature _____ Course _____

Distance _____ Time _____ Pace (mph)_____

COMMENTS _____
_____

TUESDAY

Pulse _____ Weight _____ Time _____ AM PM

Weather / Temperature _____ Course _____

Distance _____ Time _____ Pace (mph)_____

COMMENTS _____
_____

WEDNESDAY

Pulse _____ Weight _____ Time _____ AM PM

Weather / Temperature _____ Course _____

Distance _____ Time _____ Pace (mph)_____

COMMENTS _____
_____

THURSDAY

Pulse _____ Weight _____ Time _____ AM PM

Weather / Temperature _____ Course _____

Distance _____ Time _____ Pace (mph)_____

COMMENTS _____

_____

FRIDAY

Pulse _____ Weight _____ Time _____ AM PM

Weather / Temperature _____ Course _____

Distance _____ Time _____ Pace (mph)_____

COMMENTS _____

_____

SATURDAY

Pulse _____ Weight _____ Time _____ AM PM

Weather / Temperature _____ Course _____

Distance _____ Time _____ Pace (mph)_____

COMMENTS _____

_____

WEEK SUMMARY

Beginning weight _____ Time _____ AM PM

Weight loss (week) _____ (month) _____ (year) _____

Distance _____ (month) _____ (year) _____

Average daily distance this week _____ (this month) _____

COMMENTS _____

_____

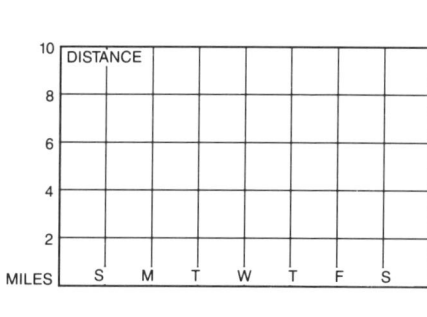

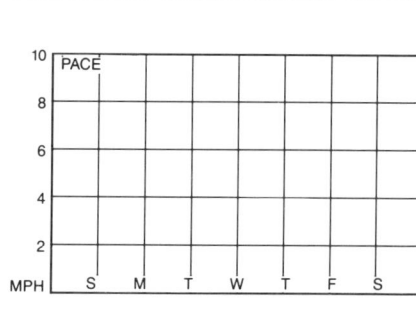

WEEK_____ 51

Goals for the week _____
_____
_____

SUNDAY

Pulse _____ Weight _____ Time _____ AM PM

Weather / Temperature _____ Course _____

Distance _____ Time _____ Pace (mph)_____

COMMENTS _____
_____

MONDAY

Pulse _____ Weight _____ Time _____ AM PM

Weather / Temperature _____ Course _____

Distance _____ Time _____ Pace (mph)_____

COMMENTS _____
_____

TUESDAY

Pulse _____ Weight _____ Time _____ AM PM

Weather / Temperature _____ Course _____

Distance _____ Time _____ Pace (mph)_____

COMMENTS _____
_____

WEDNESDAY

Pulse _____ Weight _____ Time _____ AM PM

Weather / Temperature _____ Course _____

Distance _____ Time _____ Pace (mph)_____

COMMENTS _____
_____

Pulse _____ Weight _____ Time _____ AM PM

Weather / Temperature _____ Course _____

Distance _____ Time _____ Pace (mph)_____

COMMENTS _____

_____

Pulse _____ Weight _____ Time _____ AM PM

Weather / Temperature _____ Course _____

Distance _____ Time _____ Pace (mph)_____

COMMENTS _____

_____

Pulse _____ Weight _____ Time _____ AM PM

Weather / Temperature _____ Course _____

Distance _____ Time _____ Pace (mph)_____

COMMENTS _____

_____

Beginning weight _____ Time _____ AM PM

Weight loss (week) _____ (month) _____ (year) _____

Distance _____ (month) _____ (year) _____

Average daily distance this week _____ (this month) _____

COMMENTS _____

_____

DISTANCE

10
8
6
4
2
MILES   S   M   T   W   T   F   S

PACE

10
8
6
4
2
MPH   S   M   T   W   T   F   S

 WEK _____

Goals for the week _____

_____

_____

SUNDAY

Pulse _____ Weight _____ Time _____ AM PM

Weather / Temperature _____ Course _____

Distance _____ Time _____ Pace (mph)_____

COMMENTS _____

_____

MONDAY

Pulse _____ Weight _____ Time _____ AM PM

Weather / Temperature _____ Course _____

Distance _____ Time _____ Pace (mph)_____

COMMENTS _____

_____

TUESDAY

Pulse _____ Weight _____ Time _____ AM PM

Weather / Temperature _____ Course _____

Distance _____ Time _____ Pace (mph)_____

COMMENTS _____

_____

WEDNESDAY

Pulse _____ Weight _____ Time _____ AM PM

Weather / Temperature _____ Course _____

Distance _____ Time _____ Pace (mph)_____

COMMENTS _____

_____

Pulse _____ Weight _____ Time _____ AM PM

Weather / Temperature _____ Course _____

Distance _____ Time _____ Pace (mph)_____

COMMENTS _____

_____

Pulse _____ Weight _____ Time _____ AM PM

Weather / Temperature _____ Course _____

Distance _____ Time _____ Pace (mph)_____

COMMENTS _____

_____

Pulse _____ Weight _____ Time _____ AM PM

Weather / Temperature _____ Course _____

Distance _____ Time _____ Pace (mph)_____

COMMENTS _____

_____

Beginning weight _____ Time _____ AM PM

Weight loss (week) _____ (month) _____ (year) _____

Distance _____ (month) _____ (year) _____

Average daily distance this week _____ (this month) _____

COMMENTS _____

_____

DISTANCE
10
8
6
4
2
MILES   S   M   T   W   T   F   S

PACE
10
8
6
4
2
MPH   S   M   T   W   T   F   S

Walking Bits

There are many groups you can contact for information about walking events, walking trails, and general information about walking.

The Walker's Club of America
445 East 86 Street
New York, New York 10028
This group has chapters in many cities across the US.

The Rockport Walking Institute
P.O. Box 480
Marlboro, MA 01752

Sierra Club
730 Polk Street
San Francisco, CA 94109
This group also has chapters in many US cities.

To locate a group of people who walk in shopping malls in your area, you might try speaking with one of the shop merchants. If there are no mall-walkers in your local mall, you could start a group of your own! Perhaps a merchant would let you put a sign in a shop window.

The Walking Magazine
P.O. Box 56541
Boulder, CO 80321-6541

For information on walking tours in Europe:
Butterfield and Robinson
70 Bond Street, Suite 300
Toronto, Ontario
M5B 1X3 Canada